DEREK WALCOTT: DRAMATIST
CREOLE DRAMA FOR CREOLE ACTING

Published by
Intelek International

ISBN 978-0-9564637-2-2

Cover design: Amos William Abaidoo, www.amoswilliam.com

Typesetting: Cypher Design, www.cyphergraphics.com

(cont. from back cover)

But care must be taken not to make simplistic distinctions between poetry and drama: the term"poetic justice" points to an interdependence between these genres; a continuum in Walcott's diverse creative actions; an interdependence, indeed, in every facet of his existence - as in every other human being's.

Add to the poetic justice phenomenon the biblical principle of "the word becoming flesh" (a phenomenon invoked by Davis here in her introduction) and a consideration of the art-life interplay (imitation) and correspondence, and one gets a sense of how both Walcott's plays and poems could be viewed as converging in a single "Act" (or series of acts) of salvation.

Walcott himself has spoken of his conflation of poetry and prayer. "I have never separated the writing of poetry from prayer. I have grown up believing it is a vocation, a religious vocation", he says, in his interview with Hirsch.

The "apostle"Walcott's productivity — his various dramatic and poetic epistles — can therefore be viewed as invitations to engage in a holistic (if not holy) communion.

As Davis concedes in her introduction "The transformational function of literature or art might not be such an ephemeral goal after all."

Davis is perhaps more forthright about this "spiritual" redemptive capacity of art — and literature in particular - in the first book she published in conjunction with Intelek International: "The Creative Use of Schizophrenia in Caribbean Writing".

A study of Walcott and three other Caribbean literary "apostles'" works (VS Naipaul, Edward"Kamau" Brathwaite and Wilson Harris'), that book actually derives its title from Walcott's description of his own writing in the following terms:

"...and the only way to recreate this language was to share in the tortures of its articulation. This did not mean the jettisoning of 'culture' but, by the writer's making creative use of his schizophrenia, an electric fusion of the old and new".

Interestingly, Walcott is here invoking, perhaps unintentionally, a concept of "creolization"that links it with original creation itself, as dramatized in the biblical book of Genesis.

More intriguingly still — especially if you share this writer's more than occasional indifference to distinctions that rest on the simplistic labeling of "science" as "secular"and "faith" as "religious" - these words from "What the twilight says" (Walcott's best known work of literary criticism) may be viewed as having some relation to the CERN scientists' quest for the elusive Higgs boson particle, which enterprise (drama) is a reversal, unraveling or diffusion of essentially the same kind of "electric fusion" that Walcott describes.

"Walcott seems intent on promoting versions of the Caribbean artist as the true priests in the spiritual renewal process of the region." says Davis.

But it is equally true, I think, that Walcott and Davis - like many others labouring for the spiritual renewal of the Caribbean — see all Caribbean people as being fundamentally equipped (if only at the most minute molecular, 'proton potential' level of their existence) to minister the sacraments of Caribbean redemption.There is no "clergy" and "laity" for them, at least theoretically.

This is affirmed by Davis in what can perhaps conveniently be described as the "tentative" foreword to this text. It is in fact a rather daring departure from the norms of publishing.

It is, in fact, an invitation, not commissioned but approved by Davis, and made in advance of a full reading of her thesis, for all Caribbean people — not just those making up the academic audiences for whom the thesis was originally written —to engage with her, Walcott, this writer and themselves in the "holistic communion" that this book can facilitate.

Derek Walcott: Dramatist

CREOLE DRAMA FOR CREOLE ACTING

CRITICAL ESSAYS, 2008

Viola Julia Davis

Dedication

I dedicate this work to he memory of my parents Israel and Elaine Eudora Jones and my late husband Dalton Davis.

Acknowledgements

This book has been in the making for over fifteen years.It started its life as a doctoral dissertation now it has become a book.

I wish to acknowledge the courage and bravery of my former student in accepting the task of publishing this book.It has been a long and arduous journey.Thank you Jay Campbell.My heartfelt thanks to my brother Michael Washington for the front cover art work,Joy Onyejiako, my niece for having faith in Michael's ability to inspire us with the design,Glenn and Janice Small and Gemma Murray my cousins for their efforts to have this feat accomplished.

Contents

Foreword — An invitation

This is not so much the foreword of an objective reviewer, as a former student and longstanding admirer and friend's invitation.

I do not extend this invitation having read Caribbean educator Viola Davis' study of Derek Walcott's plays. Having read little more than her introduction to that study so far, I am issuing this invitation closer to the beginning of such a reading and reviewing process. How dare I, you ask?

I dare because of my confidence in Davis. In addition to being a former student when she was a tutor in A Level English (literature) at the Barbados Community College, I have worked closely with her as an activist in that island's Pan Africanist community.

I have seen up close, her passion for and pragmatism about Caribbean people's — particularly Caribbean women's - capacity to creatively carve their own paths to authenticity.

This is the fundamental theme of her book "The Creative Use of Schizophrenia in Caribbean Writing" (2001, Bridgetown, Intelek International) which my organization published.

In fact, I think it important to say my belief in Davis' competence as an analyst of Walcott's plays is not the critical question of confidence here.

There is a more fundamental question that has to do with my confidence in Caribbean people - the primary readers for whom this book is intended — to think for themselves.

Through the publication of this book and the creation of the online forum that complements it I seek to engage with Caribbean people about the focus of Walcott's "careful passion": that focus is ourselves.

Like Davis (and Walcott) I have inexhaustible confidence in the creative capacities of Caribbean people.

This is not so much a foreword, therefore, as an invitation — an appeal, even - for the diverse, indigenous (Amerindian) African, Asian and European descended peoples of the Caribbean community to converse with Walcott, Davis, me and each other.

I invite all readers, but Caribbean people especially, to follow Davis' lead along the tantalizing thoroughfare that constitutes the Creole culture which has shaped our past and foreshadows (I believe) our destiny.

I dare to do this because like Walcott and Davis, I am a product of that people – Caribbean people – whose capacity for creativity is rooted in ageless formulations and reformulations of human narratives and ideologies.

Junior Campbell
March 2012

Introduction

CREOLE DRAMA

"CREOLE" drama is a drama that bears the special marks of its Caribbean origin and setting and embodies the hybrid nature of Caribbean history, culture and personality. This Creole reality is the result of the historical coming together of European and African values within the physical location of the Caribbean islands. The idea of "Creole" is being used to describe the result of the fusion of these three realities and this result is seen to contain a multi-cultural plentitude that is 'characteristic' of the cultural and intellectual reality of the Caribbean.

What is meant by Creole Drama is reflected in the folk drama, history plays, experimental Broadway musical plays and the author's later psychological plays, each of which sub-genre casts a slightly different light upon Walcott's concern with the nature and expression of the "Creole" reality that this text takes to be at the heart of Caribbean identity. Post-modern, Post-colonialist, Feminist and other branches of contemporary literary theory are used to comment on the works analysed, in order to demonstrate the variety and versatility of Walcott's dramatic imagination, but more importantly to make clear that contemporary theory's concern with complex, trans-cultural realities echoes the fundamental truth at the heart of Caribbean society and culture — so much so that what is meant by "Creole" comes close to embodying post-colonial theory's key concept of appropriation, hybridity, syncreticity, abrogation and the metaphor of maronage.

This text is also concerned with the language of Walcott's plays — with "Creole" language and expression and the way in which the individual 'voice' of the playwright merges with the idiom of a people to effect a subtle 'displacement' of the values and perceptions associated with the English Language in such way as to 'claim' it as a Caribbean reality. This is what the discussion refers to as the "careful passion" of Derek Walcott. The 'careful passion' of which I speak wrestles with form as Walcott confronts the rich orality of Caribbean people, their legacy of slavery, the rhetoric of Black Power and African revivals.

The focus then is on Walcott's "Creolisation" of the drama. The creolisation of European culture becomes a vehicle by which he contrives to subvert the hegemony of bourgeois culture by celebrating the reality of a Caribbean identity through the incorporation of the dialect or "nation language" as Kamau Brathwaite[1] prefers to call it. Walcott incorporates the indigenous art forms, the steel band, calypso and reggae, in examining the folk lore, the history and the psychology of the colonized. His plays embody his notion of the Adamic Vision – the task of the New World – to be creative in a new way. But this 'Adamic Vision', must, as its antithesis, reject the lovelessness of accepting history literally, of wallowing in the mud of self-pity or triumphal Africanism. It must rather assume the role of the "Beloved Son" who in love embraces all – all that the old world Euro-centric vision bequeathed albeit to his pastoral Beloved son and to fashion a Covenant with the old. This is the 'Creole' word made flesh. On this continent and in these islands of this New world; it is all synthesis, all 'Creole'. So that Henri Christophe is neither about an African Slave nor an European revolutionary, he is a synthesis of both. He is a creation. He is Creole, just as Ti-Jean is a tribute to Caribbean orality and humanism, garbed in the universal structure of the folktale, albeit a Creole creation. The Last Carnival is the Creole play par excellence, embracing not only the French Creole as 'Creole', but the culture which their forefathers brought from French Europe. O'Babylon! celebrates the Rastafarian as a uniquely Caribbean creation. The Rastafarian is the 'Creole', a synthesis formed from the validation of his Africanness and the tension which develops in response to a colonial situation which marginalizes him and his history. Something unique is born here. Walcott's 'Creole' metaphor therefore dictates form, dictates the use of the Caribbean oral tradition, while making quite extensive use of all the world's dramatic traditions.

Any critic of Walcott's work must be as catholic in the application of literary theory in the quest for understanding the plays as is the playwright himself, in his experimentation with forms. This forces the critic as it were to "try-on" the many theoretical constructs which can be tested in the process of appreciating Walcott's fascination with form.

Walcott answers the question about "Creole acting" comprehensively in the dialectical essay "What the Twilight Says: An Overture" as he discusses his experiences with the Trinidad Theatre Workshop, in which he confronts the scepticism of many, that Caribbean people can create of their collective experience, a drama.

…and now, a few would approach him with frightening requests, to understand the technique of the theatre as if it were something different from what their bodies instinctually practiced, for better speech when theirs had vigour that was going out of English.[2]

Walcott is convinced that not only do Caribbean people possess the virtues necessary for good acting, but that the inferiority complex which they inherit by virtue of their history is quite unjustified. He sets out to dispel all the fears Caribbean people possess about themselves, and about their speech, their calypsos, their dance, their steel band, whatever they have created, and moves to valorize these in his drama and his theatre company as he marshals the discourse on Caribbean man's identity as a vehicle for his drama. He pursues the notion of creolisation, that which is bred in the West Indies and nurtured, that which contains hereditary traits of both the European and the 'native' in his perception of the challenge of adapting Tirso de Molina's, El Burlador de Sevilla, The Joker of Seville, he states:

The most significant thing for me is to feel that I can adapt such a complete work without any sense of artifice. If I were living in another country or city, I might have felt I was indulging in an hierarchical literary exercise with no companionship in the body of modern theatre. But the verse play is not a literary exercise in many parts of the Third World and particularly my experience in the West Indies.

He also notes the link between the Spanish past of Trinidad and avers that Shakespeare creolised the classic theatre as much as any Third World writer who re-invents these legends which are after all universal whether they be Don Juan or Faust.

When one considers the challenging objectives Walcott set himself in his career as playwright, one has criteria to judge him by. He states:

When one began twenty years ago it was in the faith that one was creating not merely a play, but a theatre, and not merely a theatre, but its environment.[3]

It is the notion of creating a theatre's "environment" that fascinates, for surely Walcott had in mind more than "place", more than "surroundings", in his use of the word "environment"; surely he was thinking of "people", of transforming people. He seeks something as ambitious and nebulous as transforming a society.

Does Walcott expect to transform society simply by the beauty of his thoughts and language? He does espouse an "Adamic" sense of awe and wonder which good literature produces, this encourages a possibly unfounded faith in the 'transformative' power of beauty, not simply the beauty of form but the beauty of the evolving potential of the individual which literature champions. The author/artist is the creator of these delights. The transformational function of literature or art might not be such an ephemeral goal after all.

Theories on post-colonial literature are very relevant to this discussion of Creole drama, since the actual metaphor of 'Creole' which Walcott embraces presupposes the cultural mix of Europe and the New World, of Empire and Colony. The term 'post-colonial' covers all the cultures affected by the imperial process from the moment of colonization to the present day. The literatures coming out of the experiences of colonization tend to foreground the tension with the imperial power by emphasizing their difference from the assumptions of the imperial centre. It is this which makes them distinctly post-colonial. The discussion of post-colonial writing is largely a discussion of the process by which the language with its power and the writing with its signification of authority has been wrested from the dominant European culture. These are features of post-colonial societies which are common to all, themes of place/displacement, power/ powerlessness, centre/marginality, race/culture. Post-colonial literature, its theory and practice are particularly relevant to Walcott's O'Babylon!, and Franklin, but can be linked to the very metaphor of 'Creole' which propels Walcott to the centre, which can approve his work as 'British" writing.

The plays I have chosen cover a period of almost four decades (1950-1989). The earliest play is Henri Christophe, published in 1950, the latest, the unpublished Franklin (1989).*

Several of Walcott's plays are still unpublished or difficult to locate. Drums and Colours, which was written to mark the short-lived West Indian Federal experiment of 1958, is out of print at this time. The plays chosen are peculiarly representative of his oeuvre. Some of the plays have been reworked and their themes rethought. The Last Carnival began its life as the experimental In a Fine Castle (1970), a play which presented the French Creole/White element in Trinidad in confrontation with the Black Power protagonists. It underscores the untenable positions which rigid racial stances could produce in a society. It was reworked as The Last Carnival which focuses on the theme of the creolisation of European culture, a metaphor of

Walcott's vision of the Caribbean. Pantomime seems to be a refinement of the play The Charlatan whose main character was a calypsonian. Walcott seems intent on promoting versions of the Caribbean artist as the true priests in the spiritual renewal process of the region. His later plays, A Branch of the Blue Nile (1986) for example, see Walcott returning to some of his concerns about Caribbean man's unwonted inferiority complex vis-à-vis his relation to world cultures. Since this concern is well handled in Pantomime, Branch was not included for consideration in this text.

The Folkplays consist of *Ti-Jean and His Brothers* (1958), *Malcochon or the Six in the Rain* (1959) and *Dream on Monkey Mountain* (1970). These are the early plays which reflect Walcott's desire to base his drama on "unaccommodated man", the unsophisticated, simple inhabitants of the Caribbean – fisher folk, charcoal burners, labourers.

These plays probe moral, ethical and religious values. They probe challenges to be human as in Dream which questions the basic assumptions of Caribbean identity. There are other plays by Walcott involving the Caribbean "folk", but these three are chosen because they emphasize somewhat different aspects of the theme of the folk and also because they are susceptible to the different contemporary critical approaches. They illustrate the variety and sophistication of Caribbean folk themes and elements as well as the versatility of the playwright. No particular significance attaches to the order in which the plays are treated.

The historical plays are Henri Christophe and Last Carnival. Both engage us in the reality of Caribbean history. Henri Christophe epitomizes the continuing dilemma of Hayti, the first black Independent Republic of the New World. It celebrates the revolutionary struggle of the slaves against their French masters. As the first of Walcott's major plays, it is also very different from and contrasts interestingly with Last Carnival, a play that examines French cultural influences in Trinidad. The point of my argument here is that, whether the texts examine war or culture, they attempt to put in context the historical influences which determine the process of creolisation and the part it plays in Caribbean man's experience.

The experimental Broadway Musical plays considered are *O'Babylon!* (1978) and *The Joker of Seville* (1978). These are attempts at a Broadway musical genre in which the music and rhythms of the Caribbean can be experimentally incorporated; The Joker, for instance, is an adaptation of Tirso de Molina's El Burlador de Sevilla, set in a Spanish court. It is truly 'Creole' in its crossing of the Atlantic and its socialisation into Spanish Trinidad.

O'Babylon! embraces post-colonial themes of nativism and the transformation of national consciousness in the quest for liberation. Rastafarianism is examined as a metaphor of displacement. Rastafarians see themselves as displaced persons, since Africa is their true home; their struggle is the struggle to deconstruct the Imperialist structures in language and religion while foregrounding African culture. A post-colonial theoretical framework works well in discussing this play.

As "Psychological" plays I have chosen *Remembrance* (1980), *Pantomime* (1980) and *Franklin* (1989). This is in no way meant to suggest that these are the only psychological plays in Walcott's oeuvre; I have chosen these because, to me, it is in these plays that one can sense a developmental thrust in terms of the movement from "unaccommodated man" through historical influences which determine his being, through more individual interpersonal concerns and adjustments to living out the consequences of one's place in the world. Given all the determinants of place and history, how does one relate to the other, be it woman/man, or marginal/central, African/European, coloniser/colonised. One can almost see the logic of proceeding from the Broadway experimental Musical plays examining the psyche of the people on the margins of empire, thus the Psychological plays bring the sequence to a close. Yet there is a sense in which, as one moves from Remembrance to Pantomime to Franklin, it is possible to argue for a movement from healing to wholeness/health, from the colonised rejection of self to mimicry of coloniser, to acceptance of self via the process of creolisation in Franklin. There is here a notion of transcendence, a vision of wholeness, of achievement even though this notion might be superseded in the future by Walcott. I must point out that I am not here arguing necessarily for a chronological progression, but rather a thematic one. Versions of Franklin did exist long before the other two plays were written and these would therefore invalidate any notion of a purely chronological development – although I feel that the most recent version of Franklin, produced by Walcott in 1989 for the 1990 Barbados production, is sufficiently distinct from its predecessors to be considered almost a different play. In any case, my argument is meant to draw attention to the way in which certain post-colonial concerns, evident in Remembrance and Pantomime, seem to reach their farthest point of development in Franklin, even though the basic structure and plot of that play may date from the sixties and seventies.

This examination of Walcott's play benefits from the existing critical literature on Walcott's plays available to me. There is Robert D. Hamner's

Derek Walcott, *The Art of Derek Walcott* edited by Stewart Brown, in which there are two essays on "Walcott's Early Drama" by Lawrence A. Breiner and "Mapping a New Nile: Derek Walcott's Later Plays" by Lowell Fiet. *Out of the Kumbla: Caribbean Women and Literature* edited by Carole Boyce Davies and Elaine Savory Fido, contains two essays relevant to Walcott's plays: Lemuel A. Johnson's "A-being (Re)Calling the Body in (To) Question" and Sylvia Wynter's "Beyond Miranda's Meanings: UN/Silencing the Demonic Ground of Caliban's Woman". There is also Elaine Savory Fido's "Judgments on Art and the Macho Aesthetics of Derek Walcott" Journal of Commonwealth Literatures 21. No. I (July 1986) p.109-119, several articles, monographs and interviews. All the Walcott criticism reflected a practical critical approach. None attempted a textual or structuralist/post-structuralist approach to the exercise. Great emphasis was placed on the psychological, sociological and historical actualities of his work. Understandably his "works", not his "texts" as defined by structuralists were the basis of their discourse.

What Walcott discloses about his art, in his polemical dialectical essays and interviews is invaluable in terms of shedding light on his work. His famous "What the Twilight Says: An Overture",[4] which he hoped would neither be seen as 'manifesto' nor 'apologia' is an invaluable document for the Walcott scholar, so is his essay "The Muse of History", his interviews "The Art of Poetry" and "Chant of the Saint", (with Hirsch and Ciccarelli respectively), and the piece entitled "The Caribbean: Culture or Mimicry?" Another invaluable source of Walcott on Walcott are his Trinidad Guardian articles which he wrote over a period of several years.

Derek Walcott's plays are living proof of the creation of a Creole Drama. The carefulness of the passion which is manifested in his work, transforms Caribbean peoples' lives as they perceive themselves as the authors of their own destiny.

Folkplays

TI-JEAN and His Brothers (1958), *Malcochon, or the Six in the Rain* (1959) and *Dream on Monkey Mountain* (1970) reflects two aspects of Walcott's early drama, first is the desire to use as the subject of his drama "unaccommodated man", the unsophisticated, the simple fisherman, "Afa", as in The Sea at Dauphin; the labourers, "Charlemagne", "Sonson", "Popo", "Chantal" the woodcutter of Malcochon, and Makak,the charcoal burner of Dream on Monkey Mountain. This drama, Walcott felt, should be presented in the open, natural light, using the elements of the folk consciousness, the stories of devils and lost brothers, which were told in the lamplit doorways of a primitive rural island. In Ti-Jean and His Brothers vestiges of African animal fable appear in the chorus of forest creatures – cricket, firefly, bird and the spokesman frog. There was the need to be faithful to that universal structure of the folktale – the same rhythm, the three acts, the moral revelations – while at he same time using all the viable, vital elements in a play.

The second aspect is Walcott's recognition of the fact that one has to be eclectic, to select from all the ideas or insights which are of value to the dramatist, be they Greek, Japanese, African or European and, in the process, to creolise the theatre making it something nurtured in Caribbean soil. This he does by including the components of the calypso, the rich puns, metaphors and verbal play of fast-paced rhetoric (picong) with which West Indians are familiar. These elements create the environment which he hoped to create for his theatre, "a country for the journey of the soul,"[1] as he discourses on Caribbean identity.

Ti-Jean and His Brothers is thus very much in the mode of the folktale, the story of moral revelation, posing the questions: What makes one human? What qualities are important to the process of humanization? Is it brute force of intellectual posturing, or is it just plain good sense, one's ability to make congruent one's feeling nature with one's action, or the recognition of the unity of man and nature? Three brothers are pitted against the wiles of the devil to determine their humanity. I have examined this play in the context of the challenge to be human, to be creative, using a post-structuralist reading, thus one looks at the structure of the play as the conduit to meaning rather than focusing on the meaning of its work and its implication or value. The Cartesian division of the world into Ego and phenomena has had two tragic effects: one was to alienate nature from man by denuding it of human significance and thereby depriving man of his natural sense of continuity with the environing world leaving his to face the absolute alone; and the other was the delusion of intellectual pride that he was greater than the animal and natural world. This is counterposed to the mythic, the sense of togetherness and community. Caribbean people's shared history stimulates the discourse of the play. One thus contrasts two critical modes, the traditional humanist interpretation, and a critical examination by which oppositions can be partly determined or by which they can be shown to partly undermine each other in the process of textual meaning, in other words, deconstructing the discourse. One discovers in this exercise that ideology is class/culture based and that the traditional humanist approach might obscure the subtle meanings of the text, while deconstruction opens up the discourse as it confirms man's unity with all nature and his creativity. Laurence A. Breiner does go beyond the traditional-humanist approach in suggesting the reinscription of reality as the text when he states:

> In the search for the right protagonist Walcott is seeking a place for himself in the text of his island.[2]

While this may or may not be so, it does not help us very much in terms of the meaning of the play.

Malcochon or the Six in the Rain has religious, ethical and moral connotations; that is one can determine one's values and ability to make choices through the sublimation of desire and the nurturing of will power, thus one's integrity and self respect are manifested through right action as individuals in a community, in all humanity and love. The common criminal is used to invoke the notion that every man must assume the guilt of every other man's and must vicariously "die" with him every time that he misses the mark. The discourse is centred on man's penchant for missing the mark, which manifests itself in the difference between what he ought to do and what he actually does; the notion of "sinner" is thus called into question. Who is the sinner pray and who is the saint? In this play which I term a "deconstructive delight", I examine Derrida's "negative theology" and the "theology" of the play Malcochon. Derrida believes that the countervailing power of criticism is to bring the text back to a certain visibility. He is most suspicious of the 'greater details' as these are not important for him and he fears the power of the text which aspires to 'science'. He views with suspicion the structuralists' love for differences, hierarchies, like victim/slayer, sinner/saint. He looks for the gaps, the impasses, the insoluble conflict between rhetoric and thought, the "aporias" which determine the most careful textuality. Malcochon presumably addresses the theological concerns of the limits beyond which man shall not go. It is about murder, slayers and victims yet it obscures this table by presenting the twin concepts of sin as "missing the mark", having good intention while doing the wrong thing, and sin as alienation of the individual, estrangement from his fellow man, and a sense of separation from God and his good self. The theology of the play presents us with "gaps", "aporias" and impasses that apparently blur the distinction between rhetoric and thought. The murderer seems much closer to our concept of saint than sinner.

Dream on Monkey Mountain also suggests the appropriateness of a deconstructive approach. The discourse is of Caribbean identity. One is able to examine the hierarchical oppositions in the light of a dominant society which places "superior" value on certain words and concepts and, by analogy, "inferior" value on others. It is most interesting that the play is framed by a dream/vision and Makak is the figure of the dreamer, the visionary who stands in contradistinction from Lestrade. It is a useful device because Lestrade ("the straddler") is seen as one who while he embodies both cultures, rejects the "native" in him and in others like him while embracing wholeheartedly the "other" culture. Thus in the first half of the play, he is seen as the voice of the sneering Eurocentric colonial, while Makak is seen as rooted in his place, his people and his history.

The binary oppositions of Dream/Reality, White/Black, Mimicry/Originality and Mountain/Valley suggest themselves in such a way that the priority of the first term is assumed. The differences occur both within and between the hierarchical oppositions and tend to undermine the philosophy they assert, thus there is a sense in which the text attempts to hide its style in a whole structure of misleading directions.

Walcott wrote that Makak for him is the spirit of the artist, that Dream was the Theatre Workshop itself, which he created, thus the artist is the visionary, the fool rooted in his society.

What links the folkplays is the sense in which the new man of the

New World seeks to define what his being or the manifestation of his beingness must be. This elemental man, this unaccommodated man has the opportunity to define for himself, to demonstrate to himself what their philosophical content. So that he folkplays, Ti-Jean, Malcochon and Dream are part of this quest to define the New World Man. Must he be a man of commonsense? Must he be pragmatic? Must he be a man who recognizes his individuality in community? Must he be a man rooted in his place, assuming the challenge of putting down roots where he is and making the most of it? Or is he one who is forever hankering after some mythical past? What is accomplished in this text which begins with Ti-Jean and ends with Dream is that one arrives at a composite picture of what unaccommodated man can achieve, of the process of development to New World Man status, that is, a man who appreciates the opportunity inherent in beginning anew, of the value of diversity, of synthesis, of eclecticism. It suggests a man who welcomes diversity, a truly "Creole" virtue.

THE CHALLENGE TO BE HUMAN IN *TI-JEAN AND HIS BROTHERS*:
A POST-STRUCTURAL READING

Descartes' dictum "I think, therefore I am" created a bifurcation which has had two tragic effects, one was to alienate nature from man by denuding it of human significance and thereby depriving man of his natural sense of continuity with the environing world, (modern man's frenetic concern with ecology is a direct backlash of his philosophy) leaving him to face the absolute alone, and the other was, and I quote:

> . . .the delusion of intellectual pride, a re-enactment of Adam's fall and of the building of Babel.[3]

Myth on the other hand gives a profound sense of togetherness, a togetherness not merely upon the plane of intellect, as is primarily the case among fellow-scientists, but a togetherness of feeling and of action and of wholeness of living, such togetherness must have, moreover, a history. It is the shared history of Caribbean people which stimulates the discourse of this play. It is the problematic condition of man, perceived as divided, separated from the phenomenal world that myth speaks to, giving back to man a consonance and a congruence between his feelings and his actions. Walcott's early plays are mythic and archetypal, they are discourses not only on Caribbean man's condition but on the human condition. These plays added credence tot eh concept of the author-function as opposed to the author as "source of significations" which fill a work. The play fulfils the purpose of this particular discourse within Caribbean society. Thus it would be interesting to contrast a traditional thematic approach to this play as opposed to a deconstructive reading using the hierarchical oppositions of Animal/Human and Animal/Supernatural. The first terms assume priority and are the "superior" terms while the second term is the "inferior" term. It is necessary to show how a deconstructive reading undermines the philosophy which the text asserts by identifying in the text the supposed ground of argument, the key concept or promise.

The opposition between post-structuralist and traditional humanist interpretation is itself a hierarchical opposition in which the post-structuralist interpretation is arbitrarily deemed "superior" to the traditional-humanist interpretation. This course can only be justified if one is prepared to question the privileged view that there is some unquestioning meaning to which all signs point or that language is "untainted" by its play of linguistic differences, and since one is prepared to do this, the humanistic-traditional interpretation becomes the "inferior" term of the hierarchical opposition. There is no ultimate word, truth or reality which will act as the foundation of all our thoughts, language and experience, so that one cannot ignore this "excess" in language and criticism by accepting a definitive interpretation of a text, which is what the traditional humanistic interpretation is wont to do. Certain meanings are elevated by social ideologies to a privileged position or made the centres around which other meanings are forced to turn. For this meaning ever to have been possible, other signs must have already existed and some excluded. It is this exclusion to which the deconstruction of a discourse hopes to give a fair hearing. How does this "other" meaning play in terms of the ideology which is propounded? How does it level with the philosophy or the rhetoric of the text?

Laurence A. Breiner in his traditional-humanistic interpretation of Ti-Jean suggests that the play sets out to select a proper protagonist.

"Indeed, Ti-Jean could be described as a play about the selection of its own protagonist. But as that play demonstrates, Walcott is most interested in the heroic dimension of lowly characters, the extra-ordinary, ordinary people of an island like St. Lucia. Above all it is the castaway, the fisherman, the woodcutter or charcoal burner who for him represents the most isolated, most reduced, race-containing symbol, the germ both of drama and of cultural identity. These are the figures he is most attracted to (and presumably most inclined to identify himself with). In his search for the right protagonist Walcott is seeking a place for himself in the text of his island."

Some of the ideologically laden words and phrases imply an exclusion which this type of interpretation does not address, for example "proper protagonist" suggests "improper protagonist" or "improper antagonist". Who or what is this which is not addressed? "Heroic dimension" implies "unheroic dimension". Lowly characters/high characters. What is their role? Why are they "lowly"? What does "lowly" mean, simply fisherman, woodcutter, charcoal burner? "Most attracted" asks this question: to what is he "least attracted"? How would we know? Walcott is seeking a 'place' for himself. Where or what is place/no place? Thus the sense that language or meaning is fixed means that there is general agreement on terms like "lowly character" or "heroic dimension" or Walcott's search for "place".

Robert D. Hamner suggests that the themes, center on the characters' methods of resisting malignant authority in their struggle to survive and to improve their lot. He says:

> ...Whatever the levels of meaning, the play is mythic in its proportion...the devil so jaded that he can no longer enjoy his own vices, challenges three brothers to a duel of wills. The one who can move him to rage and pity will be rewarded with wealth, fulfilment and peace, failure means death and his flesh will serve as a feast for the devil.

Hamner recognizes levels of meaning, but "devil", like "God" suggests unquestionable meaning, can their meaning be challenged? These concepts are the basis of our whole system of thought and language, but such transcendental meaning is a fiction since all concepts are embroiled in an open-ended play of signification shot through with the traces and fragments of other ideas.

If one begins then on the post-structuralists' path with the hierarchical oppositions of Animal/Human one would have to identify 'animal' as the 'superior' term and 'human' as the 'inferior' element in the context of the fairytale or beast fable whose conventions include a moral element in the context of the fairytale or beast fable, distinguishing between right and wrong and the regulation of conduct. These tables are usually for human edification and learning, the animals as it were to teach humans how to behave, in the spirit of the biblical injunction 'Go to the ant thou sluggard' (Proverb 6.6). Yet this is Man, whom God made in his image and likeness and gave 'dominion over the fish of the sea, and over the fowl of the air, and over the cattle and over all the earth and over every creeping thing that creepeth upon the earth' (Genesis 1.26). one is reminded though that this was before Adam's fall from Grace. After the fall even the animals will teach him. So that the human closest to the teachings of the animals, closest to his animal nature, Ti-Jean will be the human who triumphs in the end.

"Human" will include mother and her three sons, Gros-Jean, Mi-Jean and Ti-Jean, while Animal will include cricket, frog, firefly and the bird. If we look at the relative reactions of the animals and humans, we will note that from the very beginning the animals with their ears closer to the ground, seem to possess more information than the humans. The cricket informs us that Ti-Jean's the man in the moon, while the frog tells the story of how he accomplished that feat. Ti-Jean is the boy with the faggots on his shoulder and a small dog trotting with him. He got the heap off sticks from the Devil whom he beat, for which deed God put him in the moon to be the sun's right hand and to light the dark. He relates the tale of the mother and her three sons. Gros-Jean is the oldest, the strongest and the stupidest. Mi-Jean the second, half as stupid a fisherman who loves studying books, a fisherman who so loves debates that he forgets "de, bait".

The animal as storyteller in the voice of cricket is the imaginative creative voice which discerns character differences and assigns values to them while the humans described, except for Ti-Jean, are seen as egotistical and stupid, thus the hierarchical opposition remains faithful to the rhetoric and philosophy of the text. The cricket refers to Mi-Jean, "look man who was a fool". Bird enquires about the extent of the mother's poverty and frog explains the predicament of the mother whose 'old hands dried up like claws' heaping old sticks too weak to protect her nest. He describes her little house on the brow of the mountain where it was so cold not only would the frog stop singing but all the creatures were unable to function. The cricket expresses his sympathy for the mother, so does the frog. Animals express sympathy, while the bird, incredulously, wishes to know if the family was frightened of the devil. Animal/bird is not afraid of the devil's show of power while Man/mother shows fears. Her fears are a manifestation of an imaginative assessment of the devil's potential. Since Animal/Human are both using imagination, the opposition begins to open itself up to question, the superior/inferior opposition is blurred, the integrity of the opposition begins to disintegrate.

When the animals interact with the human beings, we learn a lot more about the human beings than we do of the animals. After frog is kicked by Gros-Jean, this sends the bird, the cricket and the frog all scurrying shrieking and croaking. The bird which wondered at the humans' fear of the devil, shows a much greater respect for Gros-Jean's potential to harm them.

The old man at least feeds the birds, and the creatures creep timidly after him, only flying away as he remarks:

Eat, and eat one another! Its another day. Ha! Ha! Wah! Wah!

The Animal/Human, Superior/Inferior opposition is supported by Gros-Jean's cruelty to frog, the old man does not redeem the situation by feeding them since he imputes to them cannibalistic intent. Bird greets Mi-Jean politely, the creatures dance around him, but Mi-Jean does not appreciate their joy, their happiness, their love, their harmony, with the earth. He does not learn anything from them:

Bird you disturbing me!
Too much whistling, without sense
Is animal you are, so please know your
place.

Mi-Jean's suggestion that animal should know its place, opens up a fissure between man and animal which the animals do not accept. They accept closeness, oneness, while Mi-Jean seeks distance. Mi-Jean represents the Cartesian bifurcation of the world, which separates man from nature and gives him the delusion of intellectual pride. Mi-Jean does not exactly cover himself in glory. The cricket still speaks despite th rebuff given to Bird:

Where are you going Mi-Jean?

This is highly offensive to Mi-Jean. He sees this as presumption on the cricket's part. The frog enquires whether he is joining his brother since he is man's size now. Mi-Jean scornfully alludes to frog's ugliness.

You ever study your face in the mirror of a pool?
Bird informs Mi-Jean or Gros-Jean's fate:
Your brother is a little heap
of white under the bamboo leaves.
Cricket ponders on the "relics of success":
An arm of iron turned to rust.

Frog's incisive comment that Gros-Jean was strong but had no sense demonstrates the keenest of intellects. The creatures' second contact with Papa Bois, contrasts with the first meeting when they followed him. Now they disperse with bird's warning:

Run, Run, Papa, Papa-Bois.

The Animal/Human opposition supports the superiority of the first element 'Animal'. This is emphasized by their desire for community with humans, while both Gros-Jean and Mi-Jean emphasised division, distance. The humans remain alone, exposed separated from the natural world, weak and inferior. Mi-Jean's ugliness is not the ugliness fo the frog, but the ugliness of the world view of alienation and conflict rather than unity and community.

Ti-Jean's relationship with the animals is remarkably different from the other brothers' relationship, he sees them as compéres, as brothers, while Gros-Jean kicks the frog and Mi-Jean alludes to its ugliness. Ti-Jean's sensitivity to the frog's feelings is reflected in the comment:

Why should I laugh at he frog and his bass voice?

Here the Animal/Human opposition begins to slip with the appearance of Ti-Jean since both Ti-Jean and the animal are one, are brothers, both in intelligence and sensitivity. There is closeness here, inclusiveness, unity between man and nature and man and the animals. The phenomenal world is not separate from Egotistical Man.

Ti-Jean assures all the creatures that they have all their own beauty, he calls them friends and asks their help for directions to the devil's estate. They warn him as they describe the old man whose name is "wordly wisdom". Ti-Jean can empathise with the old man while blessing the creatures:

If he is an old man and motral
He will judge everything on earth
By his own sad experience
God bless you small things
It's a hard life you have
Living in the forest.[14]

Firefly returns the blessing and asks the bird, to sound the alarm if the old man comes through the grove, the firefly recalls the old man's words, of eating one another:

And we never eat each other for dinner
We do not do it from evil.[15]

This is an important distinction firefly wishes to make, the animals do not eat each other because they are evil, they do so from their survival instincts. The cricket tries to shield Ti-Jean from viewing his brothers' graves and wonders why he must fight the devil – the frog disagrees with Ti-Jean's adventurous spirit.

> *You know evil early, Ti-Jean's life will be simpler.*[16]

He thinks, 'Not so, Ti-Jean, not so, go back'. The Bird warns that the old man is coming, the frog offers help.

> *If you need us, call us, brother, but*
> *You understand we must move.*[17]

The bird tries to help Ti-Jean by pecking the rope to untie the faggots of the old man's bundle. When Ti-Jean burns the cane filed frog is there to sing of the plight of the "Dead Drunk" devil singing his song of lost souls – There is general rejoicing among the animals, frog spits at the Devil who curses fish, flesh and fowls. He even admits to fear, a human quality, as an insect brushes his dragonish hand. The devil loses the battle of wills and Ti-Jean demands his reward just to realise that his mother is dead, it is the frog who urges Ti-Jean to sing. The frog encourages him to show his humanity. What an opening up of the logic of the rhetoric to the discrepancies between the opposition of Animal/human, when the animal/superior element cooperates with the human/inferior, works with it and becomes one with it. There is no opposition between animal and human but co-incidence.

> *Show him what a man is!*
> *Sing Ti-Jean... Listen,*
> *All around you, nature*
> *Still singing. The frog's*
> *Croak doesn't stop for the dead;*
> *The cricket is still merry,*
> *The bird still plays its flute,*
> *Every dawn, little Ti-Jean* [18]
> *And as Ti-Jean obeys his friend the frog by singing falteringly*
> *To the door of breath you gave the key,*
> *Thank you, Lord,*
> *The door is open, and I step free,*
> *Amen, Lord...*[19]

This so moves the devil that he weeps and experiences the human emotion of pity and shared sorrow. Ti-Jean has earned his gift, would he just ask. He gives the Bolom the gift of life. Ti-Jean calls the little creatures together and implores them to unite, since together they are strong, apart all rotten. The frog praises Ti-Jean "a fool like all heroes":

> *...Loosening the rotten faggots of knowledge from old men to bear them safely on his shoulder...*[20]

It is the animals, the animal nature, the intuitive which informs the compassionate and the fearless. It is the animals which see through the hyprocrises and dishonesty of the humans. Both Gros-Jean and Mi-Jean claim to be hardworking, thinking people in the face of Ti-Jean's majestic idleness. They reject the mother's simple religious faith. they are cynical. "God forget where he put us" says Gros-Jean, while Mi-Jean finds God "too irresponsible".

In the encounter between the Mother/Human, and the Bolom/ Supernatural in which the human assumes the superior element in the opposition and the Bolom the inferior, it is the mother who appears to be victim, the powerless one while the Bolom, seen by her as the devil's advocate, assumes the role of power broker. This confuses the presumed hierarchy and creates the slippage which helps to undermine the logic of the text. The mother fears that her prayers to God are answered with Death. The paradox the 'God has sent me evil' escapes her. A not unexpected response from the older brothers is a superstitious one, the same brothers who are alienated from the mother's simple faith have faith in "fine sand" "turned skirt-hems", and "fingers formed in one crucifix". Ti-Jean fearlessly steps outside to investigate this phenomenon while the brothers cower inside with their fanciful notions. The Bolom delivers his message.

> *Send the first of your sons outside for it,*
> *They must die in that order.*[21]

The Bolom rejects the mother's plea that she has done no harm. He responds by making her culpable. Since a woman who 'called herself mother' did him harm. The mother must recognise the collective responsibility of every man and woman in the evil of the world. Human/mother decries the horrors of human life thus elevating the super-natural Bolom to a superior role. She tries to comfort the Bolom, she suggests to him that he is probably lucky that he does not have to know the horrors of human life, the disappointments, she wishes him peace and desires to give him a mother's touch of comfort simply because she is a mother. "For the sake of her kind." He shrieks in fear, he wants mortality only on the term that her sons die first. By his desire to be human, he reasserts the superior value of human

– thus Human/supernatural are no longer opposed in their validation of the worth of being human. The demon master reminds the Bolom of his mission as he proceeds to explain. He acknowledges the gentleness of the mother and recognises her suffering but proceeds to tell her of his own fate. 'Deformed past recognition', he offers to show himself to her while Gros-Jean and Mi-Jean wish to see and to reason with the Bolom, the mother cautions them that the sight of such horror would turn them to stone. The Bolom recognises the mother's love which keeps the house warm, she flings open the door for him. Human/supernatural open up to each other, erasing opposition momentarily. He describes his destructive deeds and explains that beside all these "pleasures" that he is dying to be human, The excesses of the language startle, as destructive deeds are described as pleasures. The Bolom offers the challenge of the devil to the three sons. Because of the tasks the devil assigns the brothers he is identified as the colonial master who seeks acceptance and belonging, who wishes to put on a "human face" to his subjects. Human/Supernatural, Sons/Devil, the superior element and the inferior element agree on the "face of it" that "human" is a superior value, the logic of the text is in question.

Except for the mother's courage, compassion, simple faith and love and Ti-Jean's honesty, sensitivity and easy alliance with the phenomenal world, the other ---, Gros-Jean and Mi-Jean do not measure up to the integrity of the animals. At any rate the humans are vulnerable, except for the Mother and Ti-Jean, to the wiles of the devil; this is another way of saying that the older brothers' pride is of the devil, but not as effective as the devil's pride. The animals on the other hand are not threatened by the devil, they are immune to his wiles. The "inferior" term human also supports the logic of the text for Gros-Jean and Mi-Jean but not for Ti-Jean or his mother; the superior term animal totally supports the text's philosophy. Yet the difference between the 'superior' and 'inferior' items is more in deference to the congruence between the two humans and the animals – Ti-Jean, Mother, Animals/superior element while Mi-Jean, Gros-Jean, Humans/ inferior elements are congruent terms.

The human/supernatural hierarchical opposition places the human as the superior element and supernatural as the inferior element since Ti-Jean's supernatural courage as he sings for the devil and the devil's longing for human emotions already contain the seeds of the self-destruction of that paradigm of opposition. The categories just do not hold, they are seen as a falsifying device which obscures reality and morality. If we range the humans, the mother and her three sons against the devil in its various manifestations (as old man, planter) and the Bolom, who symbolizes potential and possibilities since he is unborn and functions as Devil's messenger and mouthpiece whose life depends on other's death, what do we find?

The mother is characterised by her God-fearing nature. One notes the number of references to God which she makes to her son Gros-Jean.

> *When you go down the tall forest, Gros-Jean*
> *Praise God who make all things. . .*
> *There always is something stronger than you*
> *If is not man, animal, is God or demon.*[22]

Ti-Jean repeats her dictum. That our life is God's own and

> *To d whatever we will*
> *And love God is enough.*[23]

Her words of wisdom and good advice are seen in her grateful response to her youngest son's request for prayer.

> *Instinct by your shield*
> *It is wiser than reason,*
> *Conscience be your cause*
> *And plain sense your sword.*[24]

She never has a personal encounter with the devil as her sons do. Gros-Jean's misguided faith in his arm of iron makes him fearless, yet the strongest proves to be the weakest.

"It have nothing, I fraid; man beast or beast man." The iron in his iron arm is a metaphor for his unfeeling, impervious relationship with others. He is looking for success but when the old man comments on the pervasiveness of death, "The flesh of the earth is rotting worms". He is either too intent on his own pursuit of success to have heard the old man's remarks or he believes that they deserve no comment when he insists on being shown the way to success; the old man wisely replies he cannot tell him the way to success, he can show him one path through the forest. The old man is a master when it comes to the playful use of words tot eh "excesses" of meaning. If one is unconscious of this one can easily be led astray. He can tell/show but he opts to make a dubious difference for he really intends to show and tell. Yet the reply recognises the free/not-so-free choices man has, while one may tell someone what to do, it is entirely up to the human being to choose to do what he thinks is best for him. The old snake in the Garden of Eden no more committed Adam and Eve to act than did God who told them what to do. They chose what they wanted to do in the unchartered forest/garden of their existence.

The old man cautions patience, he asserts strength should have patience. One wonders whether this is advice for Gros-Jean or a reminder to the old man himself. Happily Gros-Jean is too busy thinking of the quickest way to what counts in the world, to heed this counsel, but the old man finds that an easy question to answer. "Money and power" he replies. Poor Gros-Jean has one interpretation/meaning of power, and that is his physical power, his 'iron fist', he cannot conceive of power in any other terms. He does not comprehend the slippery quality of language all he needs then is money. What does he do to get money? He uses his physical power to grab the old man, hurl him down and with his uplifted axe threaten to chop him and bury him in bamboo leaves just to get him to tell how he can get money. The old man reprimands him thus: 'With your arm of iron the first thing to kill is wisdom'. The old man sees himself as wisdom. He understands the power of wisdom, but recognises that any strong man can destroy the wise old man unless and except he uses his wiles. The old man is interested in disclosure/enclosure, inclusion/exclusion, me/he simple oppositions like the structuralists without himself comprehending the gaps which the post-structuralists realised could destroy and overturn the simple hierarchies. Yet his wisdom/power is for no more illustrious end than Gros-Jean's since they both wish some control over their lives whether it is through wealth or through some quality which the other possesses. The old man's use of language is to exert power, the power of establishment language as opposed to nation-language, the insight which Lestrade uses in Dream as he mimics the colonizers' language. Gros-Jean has no concept of the power of that language nor of its nuances. Thus Gros-Jean agrees with the old man's assessment, he really believes that his iron arm can kill wisdom. The old man reminds us that the devil wants help. Of course the devil wants help. The connection between killing wisdom and helping the devil supports the devil/old man/wisdom configuration which challenges the rhetoric and its questionable logic.

The contest between Gros-Jean and the old man/devil begins with Gros-Jean's observation. "The devil boasts that he never get vex." Gros-Jean is expressing knowingly or unknowingly a measure of surprise at this, since he has already shown his ability to express anger. It is almost as though whether he has consciously conceded it or not, that he has lost the contest. He gets "vex" and since this is the basis of the contest that he does not show anger his is a lost cause. We also see here the considerable slippage in terms of the characters and values between the devil, the old man, the planter, as "devil" also refers to Gros-Jean. The old man directs Gros-Jean to the white planter who will work him "like the devil", but he is sure that, that is what Gros-Jean wants – identification with the devil. The old man reminds Gros-Jean that an iron arm may rust, flesh is deciduous. Gros-Jean now that he is shown the way to success, ungratefully reminds the old man. "Next time, don't be so selfish". How he misreads the old man! "Selfish"! The old man is selfish but not in the way Gros-Jean believes, the old man always wanted to show him the way, but the old man knows the strength of patience, he also knows of direction by misdirection, so he can happily sing as Gros-Jean moves toward the forest:

> *Who is the man who can speak to the strong?*
> *Where is the fool who can talk to the wise?*
> *Men who are dead now have learnt this long*
> *Bitter is wisdom that fails when it tries.*[25]

The old man understands the playfulness of language, he knows the difficulty of a definitive interpretation. The conundrum is paradoxical and as elusive as the devil himself. He observes of Gros-Jean, "There went the spirit of war", for Gros-Jean has an iron arm and a clear explanation for everything in defense of which war are fought and might is still right. Gros-Jean's trials and tribulations over the two days, include working for this "damn white man", but he moves to work for the devil (inter alia) since that is the shortest route to success, but the deal is, should he show signs of anger first, he will be eaten. It needs to be said that it is the unpredictable, slippery quality of language which is helping to undermine or breakdown the reality it is attempting to portray. Gros-Jean fights the anger he feels by busying himself at work, he dutifully counts the leaves of the cane and then divides by the number of stalks, he catches seventy fireflies, he tries catching the goat, but the man does not know his name. He is called everything from Mac to Jo to Gros Chien, Horace, Hubert, Benton and Francis. What does it matter? What's in a name? The racist's dictum that they all look alike, might extend to giving them any name. What is the meaning of names? Isn't that the Admic vision? If the devil can be so prodigal with names, the lesson ought to be that giving things names is a privilege which must be cherished. For Gros-Jean this liberty with his name is a profoundly distressing experience. It is the Ego, Gros-Jean's alienating vision of man as separate from his environment, without the Cartesian redeeming grace of reason, which leaves him not only alone but less humane and less able to relate natural feelings to actions. It also identifies him with the devil who needs to experience feelings, emotions of pity. The devil and Gros-Jean find themselves in the same predicament, there is no opposition, simply congruence, a distortion of logic. Gros-Jean explodes, "I ent vex, I ent vex chief!" He has lost his cool and becomes a meal for the devil.

The old man greets Mi-Jean flatteringly "Bon Jour Mi-Jean, Mi-Jean le philosophe". Mi-Jean remembers his mother's words "no one can know what the devil wears". The old man continues his flattery by proclaiming Mi-Jean's renown as a jurist, a man with "the gift of his tongue"

> …*Mi-Jean, the avocet, the fisherman, the litigant.*[26]

He observes that Mi-Jean has one virtue more than his older brother, fear, and warns that nothing lives longer than brute strength except it is human cowardice. One hopes that Mi-Jean listens more closely than his brother did, for the old man is adept at using language for his own meanings, he easily links the virtue of 'fear' to 'human cowardice' a seed planted in Mi-Jean's head which might put him at a disadvantage when dealing with a master of subtlety. Mi-Jean's ambition is ultimately to become a lawyer, that weaver of words, words used to obscure rather than to clarify but first he goes to sea to become a rich captain since working the land is too hard. Is Mi-Jean ready for the "unchartered seas" of language? Might not "terra firma", difficult as he perceives cultivating it to be, give him a greater sense of direction, balance? Unlike Gros-Jean, Mi-Jean listens and responds to the old man, he is more aware of the "other" or "otherness" of oppositions, hierarchical or otherwise. He might not make such sense of what the devil says, but he at least responds. Mi-Jean's faith in book knowledge produces the startling dictum that wisdom might be a vice. This example of the slippage between word and meaning, wisdom equals vice turns logic upside down. When wisdom is seen as vice, and power is seen as iron fist, a whole system of political structure and social organisation is dismantled by language which undermines its own meaning. Separated from wisdom, Gros-Jean disdains women, believes in the devil and is determined to beat him with "silence and a smile". He expects that he will know if God exists when he meets the Devil, that in philosophy will be for him big knowledge.

Ah polarities of belief,
When the existence of one object
Compels that of the other,
Bon Dieu, what terms, what terms! [27]

Is Mi-Jean a structuralist who sees "polarities" and "oppositions" as simply relational, as giving existence to the "other", the opposite without benefit of meaning? One wishes that these words will give meaning to all Mi-Jean's audience, that there is some unquestioning meaning to which all these signs/ words can point. This language may simply signify Mi-Jean's desire to impress the old man of his "vice"/wisdom or of his vice/verbosity, meaningless signifying.

Ironically Mi-Jean valorises silence in his "Song of Silence" or "Your mouth will dig your grave". The planter will use the conflict between Mi-Jean's ostensible wish to be silent and his more virulent need to "debate" to exhibit his book learning. It is on the philosophical question whether man is better than an animal, whether animals have souls that Mi-Jean's armour of silence is pierced. One already knows the answer of his question for the "inferior" human Mi-Jean does not measure up to the "superior" animals in the hierarchical oppositions. It is so abhorrent to him that anyone could suggest equality between man and animal, that he accuses the planter of being a "crooked minded pantheist". The final straw for Mi-Jean is when the planter embraces him and recognises him as:

Descendant of the ape, how eloquent you have become! How assured in logic! How marvellous in invention! And yet poor shaving monkey, the animal in you still in evidence, that goat. . . [28]

The stupidity of Mi-Jean's wisdom is such a deconstructive delight simply because of the slippery nature of the language and its particular system of meaning. To accuse the devil of being a "crooked minded pantheist", presupposes the devil's recognition of God in everything, but is the devil/God opposition meaningful or not in this language "de-bait". Language which catches us off-guard is but a bait, a trap.

Mi-Jean loses the battle of wills by shouting in anger. "Oh shut you damn mouth, both o'all you." The old man understandably is in a triumphal mood when he crows:

Power is knowledge, knowledge is power, and
Devil devours them on the hour! [29]

His knowledge of the other two brothers assures him of a meal of the third. What is this knowledge that is so powerful? The deductive argument that since the other brothers were easily moved to anger, ipso facto, the third brother will be so moved. He anticipates a meal of Ti-Jean thus: "...tenderer than old muscle power, simpler than the net-empty atheist. For the next dish is man-wit common sense". The old man as he meets Ti-Jean is impressed with the subtlety of his speech, the devil understands very well the "excess" of language and is amazed at Ti-Jean's grasp pf the playfulness of language. Ti-Jean the youngest and most callow proves to be stronger and the most able in every way. Ti-Jean having ascertained that the old man is indeed the adversary/antagonist he suspected he was, the unmasked Devil is a trifle, a very trifle angry. Ti-Jean remarks:

> *Cover your face, the wrinkled face of wisdom,*
> *Twisted with memory of human pain,*
> *Is easier to bear; this is like looking*
> *At the blinding gaze of God.*[30]

Since literary language constantly undermines its own meaning, Ti-Jean's analogy that the devil's face is like "looking at the blazing gaze of God", is confusing simply because there is no unanimity on the meaning of God or Devil or the "blazing gaze of God". God/Devil, Devil/God are more alike than different, who knows? The old man agrees with Ti-Jean. "It is hard to distinguish us." Good and evil wear similar faces! How ironic that both the evil old man and the good Ti-Jean, enjoy the gift of subtle speech. Both the snake in the Garden and God speak with similar voices!. The devil issues the challenge to Ti-Jean to catch the goat without losing his temper. He does not lose his temper – the goat loses his 'seed'. It is altered and stays put – the creative solution, implies that one is privileged to try new paradigms, deeds not words, since words are so enigmatic, so difficult to pin down meaning. Is the whole question of meaning intertwined with deeds, with structures? Is it the construct rather than the words? Is not that the post-structuralists argument? Is that the challenge Deconstruction poses vis-à-vis the humanistic traditional interpretation?

The anger of the devil is palpable. Ti-Jean's next chore is to count all the canes, his solution simple. "Burn the cane, burn the cotton." For Ti-Jean there is a correlation between the excesses and playfulness of language/meaning/creation/construct. Manwit and commonsense can make playful connection between the Ego and phenomena, between feeling and action, a congruence which is creative and solves problems. The post-structuralists could relate to

Ti-Jean, to the Ti-Jeans of the Caribbean, the calypsonians, the dub-artistes, the reggae lyricists, who understand that language is as difficult to pindown as it is to suggest meaning out of hand without due attention to social institutions, to the Caribbean soil, and culture from which these grow.

Ti-Jean recognises that the only way to annoy the devil is to disobey him, that is to become creative, not to simply follow in the traditional paths, interpretations, ideologies of the "old men", "old orders" to forge "new worlds and new orders". The devil knows about disobedience, it was disobedience which converted his status from "Son of the Morning" and "Prince of Light" to that of "Prince of Darkness". It was Caribbean writers' disobedience to the old order, to paying obeisance to the master's text, to the hegemony of European writing that created for them the princely move from margin to centre in the literary hierarchies. The devil's anger cannot be contained when he realises that his "only house" is burnt. It is no longer one "house" of the master text, of literary achievement. The Ti-Jeans/Caribbean writers have burnt down the house while the devil rages not only against Ti-Jean but against his mother and his brothers. There is no dissimulation of his rage when he says:

> *I've been watching you, you little nowhere nigger! You little squirt, you hackneyed cough between two immortalities, who do you think you are? You're dirt, and that's where you'll be when I'm finished with you. Burn my house, my receipts, all my papers, all my bloody triumphs.*[31]

Ti-Jean's cool, calm and collected question is subtlety itself.

> *Does your master sound vexed to you.*[32]

The devil's a bad loser, he does not intend to accept defeat at he hands of Ti-Jean, he does not intend to play fair. It is the Bolom, pure potential, the symbol of all unborn creativity, all who stand on the threshold of attainment to intervene, who has to remind the devil of his bargain. Ti-Jean's supernatural courage, the ability to sing despite the despair of the death of the Mother/the Muse/the dead empire, moves the devil to human pity, and bestows the gift of life to the Bolom. The Bolom's joy at being born is awe inspiring:

> *I am born, I shall die! I am born,*
> *I shall die!*
> *O the wonder and pride of it! I shall*
> *be man!*
> *Ti-Jean my brother!* [33]

The devil never gives up, he assures Ti-Jean in parting that "the fight is still on" between good and evil, between post-structuralist interpretation and humanistic traditional interpretation, between post-colonial literature and the imperial canons. The fight for centre stage, for meaning, for empowerment is still on. This is more than a play, it is a deconstructive device aimed at undermining categories and the certainties that they represent.

DECONSTRUCTING THE DISCOURSE IN DREAM ON MONKEY MOUNTAIN

Michael Foucault suggests that literary criticism shifts its emphasis from the "themes or concepts that discourses set in motion", to the study of discourses;

> ... not only in terms of their expressive value or formal transformations, but according to their modes of existence. The modes of circulation, valorization, attribution and appropriation of discourses vary with each culture and are modified within each. The manner in which they are articulated according to social relationships can be more readily understood.[34]

Foucault, also suggests that the author's name manifests the appearance of a certain discursive set and indicates the status of the discourse within a society, but this name has no legal status nor is it located in the insights of a certain discursive construct and its very particular mode of being, so that there are a certain number of discourses that are endowed with the author-function while others are deprived of it.

The author is a certain functional principle by which, in any culture one limits, excludes and chooses, in which one may impede the free circulation, the free manipulation, the free composition, recomposition, and decomposition of fiction. In fact, if we are accustomed to presenting the author as a genius, it is because we make him function in exactly the opposite fashion. The author is an ideological product, since we represent him as the opposite of his historical real function.[35]

Thus one can critically assess Walcott's Dream on Monkey Mountain from a thematic perspective and state the plot and themes as Laurence A. Breiner does when he notes that:

> ...the plot is rudimentary; an old charcoal burner known by the name Makak brings his load down from the mountain to sell on market day. Arrested for appearing drunk and disorderly he spends Saturday night and Sunday morning in jail, then returns, to his hut on the mountain. But his behaviour is eventually explained as the result either of a fit brought on by the full moon (according to his friend Moustique), or his encounter

with an apparition, *"the moon, the muse, the white Goddess" according to Makak, and the play itself is a moon-struck dream, initiated with evocative music and mime. The body of the play, six scenes framed by a prologue and parallel epilogue constitutes an enormous multi-faceted response to a policeman's routine question: "What is your name?" But, this is only clear from the perspective of the epilogue when the moonlit prologue is recapitulated in the prose light of the sun, and Makak at last answers simply with his name, Felix Hobain.*[36]

Brenier also notes that Makak and his series of "assistants" together constitute a beast fable: mosquito, mouse, tiger along with the Caribbean macaque. He is variously identified as mimic monkey, remote mountain gorilla, King Kong. But these were the racist epithets of the colonial period. Now in the era of independence and black consciousness he is touted as King of Africa, Lion of Judah. The problem of naming raises this central question of the play: on the spectrum from ape to lion, where is the actual man? Brenier further states that Walcott, by focusing on "reduced race-containing protagonists and asking "who is he?" "what should he be called?" investigates West Indian identity. Makak is presented as a man shaped under pressure. These are the routine oppressions of a highly stratified society, in which his place is determined by race, by colour, even by language – his French patois against the English of authority. Brenier continues to explain that there is also the pressure of history with the burden of slavery and colonialism. Makak's occupation as a charbonnier provides images that suggest optimism, Moustique for example describes coal as one billion, trillion years of pressure bringing light. The implication is that in the words of Hopkins familiar to readers of English literature; "this Jack, joke, poor potsherd, patch, match-wood" can become under pressure "immortal diamond". Finally, he states that in these images, Walcott cannot entirely suppress the implication that black coal improves by becoming "white" among other things and that the other paradox associated with the apparition reflects one of the burning issues of the years around 1970: whether West Indian identity was to be rooted in the Caribbean or in Africa.

This is Brenier's thematic criticism of Dream on Monkey Mountain. A deconstructionist's approach would disassociate the author's name from the text, since it is not located in the fiction of the work, but would instead note the author-function of the discourse. Foucault's concern is with the control exerted by a society and the process whereby this control is exerted, since control cannot always display itself nakedly, it has to disguise itself by the language of truth, discipline, rationality, utilitarian value and knowledge. It is the process of isolating, excluding the opposite, the language of the governed that is the machinery of corporeal and mental control, the language of controller/controlled is a language of hierarchical oppositions, some words/ concepts are "superior" while the opposites are "inferior". For example in the hierarchical oppositions of positive/negative, "positive" is the superior" term. To understand how the hierarchical oppositions operate in terms of deconstructing a discourse, it is necessary to show how deconstruction:

> *...undermines the philosophy, the philosophy it asserts, or the hierarchical oppositions on which it relies, by identifying in the text the rhetorical operations that produce the supposed ground of argument, the key concept or premise.*[37]

In this deconstruction, the text is supported by Jacques Derrida's definition, that a text is only a text if it conceals from the first glance, from the first comer the law of its composition and the rule of the game. Dream on Monkey Mountain will prove to be a text which can be read without reference to the author's name. One also wonders whether a text is as essential for the play's realization in the same way as with a novel or a poem, especially since Walcott has more than one text for some plays. The key terms 'Dream', 'Monkey' and 'Mountain' readily present themselves in the creation of hierarchical oppositions. Reality/Dream, Creativity/Mimicry, Mountain/Valley. Yet our hierarchical oppositions must necessarily begin with the Prologue/Epilogue, the play format which informs the form/ content of the play. The prologue and epilogue frame The Dream play. This form dictates that the contents of the play – the play itself – is a dream. Other oppositions which suggest themselves are Spiritual/Material; Human/ Animal, and finally the truth/deception opposition would determine how far the author-function has fulfilled its Anacncy-trickster role in hiding the real intention of the text.

The prologue establishes the tone of the discourse and introduces the main players. Corporal Lestrade, a mulatto prison officer, is interrogating the old man Makak, a Charcoal burner. He is in jail for damaging Felicien Alcindor's shop while in a drunken state. He is accused of blasphemy, sedition, urging destruction of Church and State. He claims among other things that he was the direct descendant of African kings, and that he has had an encounter with a woman "The loveliest thing I see on this earth". Corporal Lestrade, interlaces his charge with questionable erudition and racist stereotypes of black people. Witnessing Lestrade's tour de force are two thieves Souris and Tigre who ironically applaud Lestrade's performance. The corporal awaits the prisoner's response to the question, what is your name?

The epilogue supplies the answer – Felix Hobain, alias Makak, who is about to leave the jail after spending Saturday night experiencing what his loyal friend Moustique terms "a rough night". Moustique has been searching for his friend and will accompany him home. Makak is happy to be going home, to a place where men can look up and say:

Makak lives there. Makak lives where he has always lived, in the dream of his people.[38]

The Reality/Dream binary opposition is relatively obvious. Creativity/ Mimicry owes its designation to the connotation of Monkey/Mimic and the opposite of Mimicry is Creativity, Mountain/Valley come with a proviso. "Mountain" is used in the context of a transcendental experience, as the late Martin Luther King uses the expression in his famous 'I have a dream' speech. He uses both items 'dream' and 'mountain'. Dream is used as "envisioning", "hoping", "expecting", "prophesying" while the "mountain top" experience as in "I have been to the top of the mountain" where "Mountain" is filled with Biblical connotations of a transcendental Nature, Moses, Jesus Christ, Makak experience this phenomenon. If one accepts the hierarchical oppositions Reality/Dream, Creativity/Mimicry, Mountain/ Valley, Spiritual/Material, Human/Animal and truth/Deception and the theory of the priority of the first term and conceive of the second term in relation to it as a complication, a negation, a manifestation or a disruption of the first, one may be in for an interesting interpretation of the text.

When Corporal Lestrade says:

Animals, beasts, savages, cannibals, niggers, stop turning the place into a stinking zoo![39]

This outburst for him is the reality of people who have not yet become homo-sapiens, of sub-humans, but this imagery is a projection of a racist reality which questions the humanity of 'niggers' since the rhetoric locks them into the same category as animals, and houses them in a place designated "zoo" for viewing. On the other hand "savages", "cannibals" and "niggers" are human but depraved humans, uncultivated, uncivilized, or more kindly, primitive humans, used not in the sense of early, ancient, simple, old fashioned but in the pejorative sense. People who eat other humans, animals feeding on their own species. Animals, beasts, savages, cannibals and niggers are used as equivalent terms. The reality is that Lestrade is the zoo-keeper, the person who lives in a symbiotic relationship with his charges. He depends on them the way cannibals feed on their own species. Lestrade is also a very literal man, he is presiding over the animals – Souris, Tigre, Moustique and Makak – mouse, tiger, mosquito and monkey.

Makak is a dreamer. To be a dreamer is a very human quality. He dreams therefore he is. He imaginatively soars beyond his present reality of drunken charcoal burner to a sense of his majesty, his kingship.

> *Lady in Heaven, is your old black warrior*
> *The King of Ashanti, Dahomey, Guinea,*
> *Is this old cracked face you kiss in his sleep*
> *Appear to my enemies, tell me what to do?* [40]

The transcendent quality of Makak's rhetoric, "Lady in heaven", and the affirmation of kingship, markedly contrast with Lestrade's "savages, cannibals, niggers". There is a sense of worship and adulation, power, love and authority in the rhetoric.

"Is this old cracked face you kiss in his sleep." The appeal of this vision, this "Lady in heaven" to confound his enemies, to avenge him is linked to the royal rage, the rage of the lion. Thus Makak is seen in his majesty as a thinking, feeling, wishing, supplicating entity, one who rages, loves and is filled with doubt. Lestrade sees no contradiction in Makak's definition of himself and his definition of Makak when he says:

> *Dat, you mange-ridden "habitual felon, is the King of Africa,"* [41]

and yet he is unable to shift his perception of Makak beyond that of zoo inmate. Makak wears the authority of presence, he is making clear to us revealing to us what is present in his consciousness, what he has in mind, as does Lestrade. Clearly Lestrade's role and language fit Foucault's concept of the way society sets out to control and to exclude by using language to disguise its designs, this tends to valorize its authority. If authoritative figures use the language of denigration, it is that they are part of the controlling structure which relegates and isolates and excludes the governed. It is the essence of the colonial discourse. It is the continuing discourse on Caribbean identity, it is peculiar to post-colonial societies.

Lestrade functions both as an authority figure and the voice of the Reality element in the binary opposition of Reality/Dream. Yet since "Reality" is seen as the "superior" term in the hierarchical opposition Reality/Dream and "Dream" as the "inferior" term, the complication, the negation or a disruption of the first; paradoxically it is the "superior" term

"Reality" which connotes a negation, an error, a denigration in terms of Makak's existence while the inferior term "Dream" connotes the positive affirmations of Makak's humanity. Deconstructive readings undo narrative schemes by focusing instead on internal difference. Is the Reality/Dream opposition not illusory? Lestrade refers to Makak as "de King of Africa" however disparagingly while Makak sees himself as the "King of Ashanti, Dahomey, Guinea". So that the idea of difference is an illusion. There is only the reality of the new Lestrade. Lestrade's conversion to Makak's vision, when he becomes King Makak's minister and takes up the cause of the black man, is a Reality. He seeks Makak's forgiveness thus:

> *Allright. Too late have I love thee, Africa of my mind, sero te amavi, to cite Saint Augustine who they say was black. I jeered thee because I hated half of myself, my eclipse. But now in the heart of the forest at the foot of Monkey Mountain I kiss your foot, O Monkey Mountain. I return to this earth, my mother. Naked, trying very hard not to weep in the dust. I was what I am, but now I am myself. Now I feel better. Now I see a new light. I sing the glories of Makak! The glories of my race! ...Makak! Makak! Forgive me old father.*[42]

At the same time, Makak's vision fades and he is no longer the king whom everyone responded positively to. He says:

> *...I was among shadows. Either the shadows were real and I was no king, or it is my own kingliness that crashed the shadows. Either way, I am lonely, an old man again.*[43]

Has Lestrade embraced Makak's world view? Is he now a lover of "Africa of my mind" rather than a jeerer? Does he now see the light? Does he truly embrace Makak's vision as he sings the glories of Makak? Is this conversion real? Is this Reality?

Is Makak no longer king in the Africa of his mind? Does he embrace a greater idea of kingliness? Does this idea recognise the power of his existence in this place where he finds himself? At any rate he recognises one particular reality, that he is a lonely, lost old man.

Does that make Lestrade's reality the "superior" item in the hierarchical opposition to Makak's fading dream? I would suggest not. Both Lestrade and Makak represent reality. Thus, the opposition between reality and dream fades.

In the binary opposition of Creativity/Mimicry, Creativity functions as the "superior", "essential" element of the hierarchy. Makak is the primeval, original man, he is clearly defined as such:

I remember, in my mind, the cigale sawing sawing wood before the woodcutter, the drum of the bullfrog, the blackbird flute, and this old man walking, ugly as sin, in a confusion of vapour, till I feel I was God self, walking through cloud, in the heaven of my mind. . .[44]

It is in this veritable Eden, this pristine world that Makak can create his own world. He is the New World man who can give things their names, who can name and rename and renew himself in an original way. Adam/Makak is given his name here. He is a new creature. His muse "this woman, the loveliest thing I see on this earth", this is his inspiration, his genius can flourish in this brave New World. This symbol of creativity is opposed to the mimicry displayed by Lestrade as he clothes himself in, and assumes the mantle of western culture.

My lords, behold! Behold me flayed and dismayed by this impenetrable ignorance! This is our reward, we who have borne the high torch of justice through tortuous thickets of darkness to illuminate with vision the mind of primeval peoples, of backbiting tribes! We who have borne with us the text of the law, the Mosaic tablets, the splendours of marble in moonlight, the affidavit and the water toilet, this stubbornness and ingratitude is our reward! But let me not sway you with displays of emotion, for the law is emotionless.[45]

Lestrade, the mulatto, himself a straddler between the African and European worlds, becomes the European and bear the burden of the colonizing white man, the responsibility to "civilize" "primeval peoples". He claims the fruits of Western Culture – justice, law, religion, architecture, modern technology, all these gifts which the 'impenetrable ignorance" of the primitive are unable to profit by – yet he is simply mimicking an attitude, parroting a Eurocentric view of "primeval peoples" and European achievement. In parroting the language, he exposes his acceptance of the superiority of the Eurocentric view of the world, while exposing his very rudimentary acquaintance with what he espouses.

My noble judges, when this crime has been categorically examined by due process of law, and when the motive of the hereby accused by whereas and ad hoc shall be established without dichotomy and long after we have perambulated, through the labyrinthine bewilderment of the defendants' ignorance let us hope that justice, whom we all serve, will not only be done, but will appear, my lords to have itself been done. . .Ignorance is no excuse. This is the prisoner. I will ask the prisoner to lift up his face.[46]

This mimicry is in ironic contrast to Makak's quintessential originality and creativity, yet Makak connotes monkey/mimic. Again, one sees the subversion of the hierarchical oppositions, since it is the Makak/mimic who is identified as original and creative and Lestrade who represents mimicry. Thus the "superior" element of the oppositions Creativity/mimicry, undermines the philosophy it asserts. Is it to Makak that the words of the chorus of singers are directed?

> *Everything I say this monkey does do,*
> *I don't know what to say this monkey won't do.*
> *I sit down, monkey sit down too,*
> *I don't know what to say this monkey won't do.*[47]

The difference that runs through Dream on Monkey Mountain is not located between creativity ad mimicry, it is that element within creativity which functions as mimicry, it is that element of mimicry which prevents us from ever facing up to whether what we censure coincides with what we understand. Makak's identification with originality and creativity functions as mimicry since this quest for newness, beginnings, roots and rootedness is common to all people. "I feel I was Godself" signals Makak's understanding of himself as co-creator with God? And aren't we all? What do we understand by Lestrade's mimicry? Does his valorisation of western civilization, its' law, religion, technological achievements, indeed western culture in general, and his emphasis on the ignorance of the "primeval peoples", prevent us from understanding his mimicry, his yearnings? Is the Lestrade who mouths racist slurs at Makak and the Lestrade who valorises western civilization not the same Lestrade who can be converted to Makak's view of the world, simply because he lacks imagination and the creative vision. In this crumbling of the binary oppositions through the pressure of irony and subversion, the weakness of the construct is exposed, that is the polarization, the form or structure of opposition itself, and consequently the failure to narrative coherence. From a deconstructive point of view such a basic device of narrative discourse is in itself being called into question in terms of its capacity to convey meaning.

In the mountain/valley hierarchical opposition the "mountain" is the privileged element. Makak lives there!

> *God bless you both, Lord I have been washed from shore to shore, as a tree in the ocean. The branches of my fingers, the roots of my feet, could grip nothing, but now, God, they have found ground. Let me be swallowed up in the mist again, and let me be forgotten, so that when the mist open, men can look up, at some small clearing with a hut, with a small signal of smoke, and say "Makak lives there. Makak lives where he*

has always lived, in the dream of his people". Other men will come, other prophets will
come, and they will be stoned, and mocked and betrayed, but now this old hermit is going
back home, back to the beginning, to the green beginning of this world. Come, Moustique,
we going home.[48]

Certainly Makak's sense of "rootedness" or "grounding", of home and "home coming", is underscored by the sense of his place in his people's consciousness, "Men can look up" to where he reigns in his consciousness. His unconscious identification with the Christ figure, the correspondence with the "mocked betrayed" Saviour is revealing. His is the way of salvation. He returns to an original state, to the "green beginning". Is there something about Makak's transcendence that is evergreen, that always returns to source, that always presupposes endless beginnings? Is a transcendent consciousness a well, perpetual inspiration, always fresh, always new? Makak has to be seen both as charlatan and as signifier — as the creative artist — note his "smoke signals", he is the wielder of words. He is drunkard and felon, lion and king. This can only be for moral, aesthetic and spiritual reasons that challenge and negate the colonial authority. To the extent that the other perspective, that is Makak as healer/lion/king, is contained within a dream, and not a reality, it is able to subvert the colonial reality and discourse without becoming itself established as absolute and exclusive authority. The whole paradigm of authority is undermined, the authority of the text, the authority of the discourse, as the "aporias" of deconstruction tend toward the self-destruction of the edifice of discourse. The theory of deconstruction itself become a technique of post-colonial literature, questioning all authorial and cultural hegemony.

The valley opposition, which sees Lestrade's consciousness of life as a prison underscores the self-deconstruction of the structuralist's position:

Here is a prison. Our life is a prison. Look, is the sun.[49]

Lestrade lacks the sense of freedom, home and rootedness which Makak accepts. His is an "imprisoning vision of life". He is limited by having to live within the circumscribed field of his uncreative mimicry, and must accept the choice he makes, what he "has in mind", it is his authority of presence, since the meaning of an utterance is what is present to the consciousness of the speaker. He lives this consciousness of "niggers, cannibals, savages", and has imprisoned himself in this view of the world. Even when he says, "Look, is the sun", he states a fact, he is not inspired or lifted up, he lacks connection to anything but the most prosaic — prisons, for example. He is a spectator of life with a view from behind prison bars. He is not part of a community. He excludes and is excluded. How different from Makak's inclusive "men can look up", he includes all men, has a sense of community of belonging, of caring and concern.

It is not so much the difference between the hierarchical opposition of mountain/valley, so much as the difference within the element "valley" for Lestrade presumably directs his negative view of the world in an "inclusive" way when he says "our life is a prison", but this inclusiveness is unlike the inclusiveness of Makak's "men can look up" meaning that men can aspire to something, while Lestrade's "our life is a prison" is a personal view which presumes some general acceptance. Given a choice between the view that "men can aspire" and "our life is a prison", both inclusive in intention, it is not over-optimistic to expect that more people will choose Makak's view, or hope one day to break out of prison, if Lestrade's view is embraced. Makak's view is the view of the healer, the whole person. The transcendent dreamer is thus valorised, the "superior" element, mountain, undermines the logic of the rhetoric which might seek to isolate the charbonnier Makak as a mad old man, while the corporal, the colonial authority figure of Lestrade, who wears the mantle of western culture, is only acceptable or credible in his own eyes.

The spiritual/material hierarchical opposition is represented by Makak/Moustique. Makak represents the spiritual while Moustique represents the material. The "material" is the "inferior" item while the spiritual is the "superior" item. Moustique promotes Makak thus; "The man is God's messenger". This statement precedes Makak's new role as healer, while the rejoicing is taking place over the healing of the sick man. Makak, the healer, is the wholesome exponent of the creative principle which has healing powers. Moustique intends to profit off his friend's Gift, his powers:

> *So, further the cause, brothers and sisters.*
> *Further the cause,*
> *drop what you have in there.*
> *Look! Look! Josephus walking.*
> *Next thing he will dance.*[50]

And he opens his haversack and holds it before him to collect cash/ and/or kind from the crowd. Moustique unabashedly sees himself as the Secretary/Treasurer in the Makak/Moustique partnership. He carries the "bag". Not by chance does he bear the imprint of the "Judas" figure, ready to betray his "Saviour through this love of money". "Nothing is for free" he mutters. He collects among other things the tall hat of Basil, the symbol of death who ironically states, "only a black hat, in exchange for a life". When he stops to take the coat off Basil's back, he barely interrupts his counting of the loot to hear the veiled threat of Basil.

You are standing in the middle. A white road. With four legs. Think what that mean, friend. I can wait for my hat.[51]

Moustique moves from betrayer to impostor. The opposition of Spiritual/Material, Makak/Moustique is blurred as Moustique actually seeks to transform himself into Makak, albeit a materialistic one. Moustique's death destroys the opposition and betrays the artificiality of a structure which could separate the spiritual from the material, creativity from its creation. Moustique's borrowed power and fake healing is akin to the borrowed power and fake integrity of a language which is not one's own, as Lestrade's or of a literature which does not reflect the genuine experience of a people, which is willing to profit from the soulless mimicry of a master style. Moustique pretends to espouse Makak's dream of returning to Africa and seeks "Cash from his audience".

So children of darkness, bring what you can give, make harvest and make sacrifice, bring whatsoever you have, a shilling, a yam, and put here at the mouth of God. . .[52]

It is in his attempted metamorphosis into Makak the healer, and one who reveals that the cure which his healers need is within them, 'the cure is in yourself', that he feels the spider on his hand. Before he could recover from the encounter and deny his fear, Basil exposes him as an impostor. Moustique derides the people's faith which has brought them no change. He reasons if they could believe all the Gods which have promised as much why not believe him. When this betrayal of his friend is revealed, the crowd ironically responds with the same response that the other crowd gave to their Saviour, Jesus Christ. When the crowd recognises its gullibility it is with a sense of shame that they wish to destroy this impostor, whom they had accepted as the genuine article for so long. Makak's desire to know what a dying man sees elicits this response from Moustique. "I see a black wind blow. . .A black wind." Thus the dying order, the dying empire, sees the rise of the black writer, blowing in from the margins to the centre of world literature.

It is Makak who finds worth in the deformed, drunken Moustique and gives him a sense of belonging. It is the Dreamer, who sees the worth of the people, the worth of unaccommodated man. Moustique recognises Makak's ability to inspire "a breakfoot nigger" and yet he never quite believes in his intrinsic worth. Makak on the other hand receives his inspiration from his self-acceptance, despite the fact that he is physically ugly, so much so that he would not even look at his reflection in a pool – he stirs his hands "to break up my image". Yet, walking closely to nature on Monkey Mountain he feels like "God" 'In the heaven on my mind'. He recognises his creative potential. He has a mission from God no less:

> *Like the cedars of Lebanon,*
> *like the plantains of Zion,*
> *the hand of God plant me*
> *On Monkey Mountain.*[53]

In recognizing the power of the mind, the creative potential inherent in every human being, he tells Souris, when he questions him on how he will get to Africa:

> *...The mind, the mind. Now, come with me, the mind can bring the dead to life, it can go back, back, back, deep into time. It can make a man a king, it can make him a beast.*[54]

Spiritual/Makak is closer to material/Moustique at this point than any other moment, king or beast, spiritual or material – all emanate from one mind. Moustique recognised the role of choice in human nature and he did say, "the cure is in yourself". When Material/Moustique takes on the persona of Makak, he becomes fused as Material and Spiritual the material becomes an illusion and the Spiritual/Makak becomes the reality. They are really not so much in conflict with one another as much as one proceeds from the other. The transformative power of spirit produces matter; Makak transformed Moustique by his faith in him. This inspired Moustique to have faith in himself. It is this rather than faith in the material which would have sustained his life. Instead he dies because of his faith in matter, the material – a poor substitute for the spiritual. He has betrayed and exploited the people mimicking the colonial masters' role of exploiter/exploited. He dies by the hand of the people who will not tolerate exploitation from their own.

Souris and Tigre bear the same relationship to the Spiritual/Material as do Makak/Moustique. Although both Souris and Tigre are thieves, Souris possesses redeeming features which contrast with Tigre. Souris recognises Makak as a Saviour of sorts, since now, because of Makak, he believes he is better than he was. Tigre can only rise to a deprecating sneer when Makak proclaims his knowledge of fire and wood.

You crazy ganga-eating bastard, I want meat. Flesh and blood. Wet grass. Come on, come on, show us the way to Monkey Mountain. The corporal hunting us.[55]

He engineered the jail-break for the express purpose of following Makak to Monkey Mountain to rob him of money he presumes Makak has. Makak describes him as

. . .a man who know how to hate, to whom the life of a man is like a mosquito, like a fly.[56]

On this assessment Makak makes him a general in his army. He understands the depth of Tigre's exploitive nature when the Tigre threatens him.

Money. . .that is what you wanted? That is what it is all about. . .money?[57]

Tigre, like Moustique, dies in his quest to embrace the material, to make it their sole reference point, and in so doing to deny their humanity, their spiritual nature. In the spiritual/material binary opposition Makak/Spiritual and Souris/Spiritual, the "superior" elements live on while Moustique/Material, Tigre/Material, the "inferior" elements, die, are destroyed, their faith in the material having betrayed them.

It is on the marginal elements that hierarchies depend, and it is probably useful to examine the human/animal opposition, Lestrade stands in contradistinction to the "animals" – Souris (Mouse), Tigre (Tiger), Moustique (Mosquito), Makak (Monkey), Lestrade/Human seems remarkably one dimensional when contrasted with the "animals". He is invariably disparaging, insulting and condescending. They are either "mange-ridden", and turn a place into a "stinking zoo", he recognizes Makak as a "tame and obedient animal", yet there is no milk of human kindness in his invitation to eat: "Is chow time, King-Kong, Hey Food, Food, old man".

The animals on the other hand exhibit remarkably human qualities, Souris, the mouse is compassionate and sensitive about the plight of Makak – He sees "Majesty" in Makak and advises him of his legal rights. Souris is seen by Makak as "the gentle rat" – He has faith in a God who will provide, and recognizes in Makak someone who can inspire his fellowman. Souris is not above flattery. Makak is a "blessed Saviour", nor is he ashamed of his fear, "God was like a big white man. A big white man I was afraid of". Neither is he above seeking revenge on Lestrade:

…So how it feel to be a nigger corporal? Animals. Savages! Niggers! Stop turning the place into a stinking zoo. Who is the monkey now, Lestrade? You bitch! I long had this for you.[58]

Tigre, the other thief is sneering, cajoling, wheedling and manipulating. He is insolent, ruthless and is the supreme opportunist. He plots to escape prison with Makak's unwitting help and hopes ultimately to kill Makak for money he believes the old man possesses. He's eventually killed by Lestrade. Yet it is Tigre's assessment of Lestrade that is so penetrating and illuminating, that makes him most human in his insights:

…Corporal Lestrade, the straddler, neither one thing nor the next, neither milk, coal, neither day nor night, neither lion nor monkey, but a mulatto, a foot-licking servant or marble law? He cause Moustique to die.[59]

This Lestrade defies meaning, defies definition. As a construct he is indefinable, there are no oppositions which hold fast, there is no point of reference which sticks, no prior term which determines status. He is neither one thing nor the other. He is all flux, as meaningless, and unstructured a proposition as the sterile output of the fencesitters who spinelessly kill off the impostors of genuine style.

Moustique, the self denigrating, self-hating pragmatist who parasitically profits from Makak's healing power and impersonates him for his benefit, cannot ultimately be saved from death by Makak. While his cynicism retards his development, he remains sceptical of Makak's African dream, and he it is who finally recognizes the transformation in his Saviour Makak at his deceptive apotheosis and condemns him in the crowning irony of the play.

That is not your voice, you are more of an ape now, a puppet. Which lion?[60]

Makak, the monkey, is seen as a visionary, a healer, a saviour on the one hand, and on the other, an ugly charcoal burner and charlatan, given to fits and drunkenness, not above going on a rampage every now and again but he knows that he is responsible only to God. "God's warrior", he knows that the mind can make a man a king or a beast. He majestically sees himself as 'The King of Ashanti, Dahomey, Guinea'. Human/Lestrade, because he is human undergoes a transformation and receives this accolade from Makak. 'Now he is one of us.' Human/Lestrade becomes what he once rejected, disdained, he becomes one with his animal nature. Since the hierarchical lines are blurred and the differences disintegrate, the philosophy of absolute meaning crumbles offering a partial, and tentative comment on aspects of the colonial situation, while undermining colonial authority.

In the apotheosis scene, Makak in triumph is acclaimed by a procession of warriors, chiefs and his wives. He is the conquering king of Limpopo, eye of Zambezi, blazing spear:

> *Who drew the thief to his bosom,*
> *The murderer to his heart,*
> *Whose blackness is a coal,*
> *Whose soul is a fire,*
> *Whose mind is a diamond,*
> *Dispenser of justice,*
> *Genderer and nourisher to a thousand wives,*
> *Praise him!* [61]

If Makak's canonization is achieved at the expense of killing off all that is white or Eurocentric then Makak has truly betrayed the creative vision, the dream. He destroys the power to heal, to make whole which he possessed while rooted in place and accepts both the straddlers, who mimic what they do not fully comprehend, as well as give value and worth to the drunken, the deformed, embracing the shadow side, the woundedness of the whole colonial experience.

Moustique, the animal is the "superior" element in the Man/Animal opposition as Makak the Man is the betrayer of the dream. The slippage in language occurs as Moustiqe/animal/betrayer/Makak/Man/Betrayer defies the logic of the rhetoric. When Makak says "My hatred is deep black, quiet as velvet", Moustique accuses him of mimicry. This is not the Makak he knows for he sees and hears his conversion. Has the Dream/reality been reversed? Or has the new binary opposition Truth/Deception come into play? An apotheosis is a deification, a canonization, a deified ideal, but what one sees of Makak is now a demonisation, there is no creativity in his bloodletting. When Corporal Lestrade convinces him that his Muse must be beheaded, that he must kill the "white witch":

> *. . .the mother of civilization and the cofounder of blackness. I too have longed for her. She is the colour of the law, religion, paper, art, and if you want peace, if you want to discover the beautiful depth of your blackness, nigger chop off her head!* [62]

As Makak complies he proclaims his freedom, "Now, O God, now I am free". Where is Makak, the healer, the Saviour, the compassionate one? Where is the Spiritual/Makak, the Creative/Makak, the Transcendent/

Makak? What is the Truth? What is deception? The epilogue convinces us that we have been deceived. We have been dreaming and yet the greater deception would be to ignore the truth of the rhetoric. Deconstructing the discourse in Dream lends credence to Derrida's view that all texts attempt to hide this almost androgynous style in a whole structure of misleading directions to the reader.[63] On the other hand the theory and practice of deconstruction can be seen as a post-colonial technique, a way of writing back that questions all authorial and/or cultural hegemony, whether it is the hegemony of the African presence in the Caribbean or the hegemony of European culture, or of the canonical works. Deconstruction unravels the neat hierarchical oppositions, and opens up the discourse to several interpretations, since the language of the texts give meaning a nebulous quality. Is the discourse centred on Caribbean identity and Caribbean cultural accretions? Is the discourse centred on the visionary or the Dream state? Is the discourse centred on Caribbean creativity or Caribbean Mimicry? It could be seen as all the above and yet we are never sure in which direction the text leads us, but we are all the richer for the rhetoric.

The Marriage of Derrida's "Negative Theology" with the Theology of *Malcochon, or the Six in the Rain*: A Deconstructive Delight

Said says of Derrida that he works more in the spirit of a kind of negative theology. The more he grasps textuality for itself, the greater the detail of what is not there for him – since I consider his key terms dissemination, supplement, pharmakos, trace, marquee and the like to be not only terms describing "la dissimulation de la texture", but also quasi-theological terms ruling and operating the textual domain his work has opened.

In terms of both dissimulation of the text and quasi-theology, nevertheless, the critic challenges the culture and its apparently sovereign powers of intellectual activity, which we may call method when in dealing with texts these powers aspire to the condition of science. The challenge is delivered in characteristically large gestures of differentiation. Derrida refers everywhere to western metaphysics and thought.[64]

It is the mistrust and the suspicion with which Derrida views texts that puts him on guard, as it were, against a conspiracy to dissemble, to hide its motives, and since Derrida the philosopher identifies with metaphysics and its hierarchies, he is also conscious, as is Foncault, that:

> *...the text is part of a network of power whose textual form is a purposeful obscuring of power underneath textuality and knowledge (savoir).*[65]

Therefore the counter-vailing power of criticism is to bring the text back to a certain visibility; what Derrida is most suspicious of is, the greater detail that is not relevant and the large gestures of differentiation which he espouses. In other words in the difference, in the hierarchies there are also the "gaps", the impasse, the insoluble conflict between rhetoric and thought, the "aporias" which undermine the most careful textuality. It is these spaces which conspire to destroy the façade of the authority of the text and the hegemony of western culture, thus the deconstructive literary technique fuses well into such an anti-establishment text as Malcochon, or the Six in the Rain, where the possibility of absolutes, whether of truth of meaning crumble.

Malcochon presumably addresses the theological concerns of the limits beyond which man shall not go. It attempts to examine the twin perceptions of sin as "missing the mark" on the one hand by having a good intention and doing the wrong thing, and alienation, the separation of the sinner from God, community and self, on the other. It suggests that the crux of the dilemma is that sin, whichever perception of it one chooses, causes alienation of the individual, estrangement from his fellow man and a sense of separation from God, his good self. Hamner, summarizes the play thus:

Malcochon, subtitled The Six in the Rain, carried a epigraph from Sophocles: "who is the slayer, who the victim? Speak". The characters introduced by the storyteller, the Conteur, include the old man, Charlemagne and his nephew Sonson; Popo and his wife, Madeline; then the aged woodcutter Chantal with his companion, a deaf-mute called Moumou. Because Chantal (the slayer-victim of the epigraph) is old, ugly, and a feared criminal, he stands as a test case for Ti-Jean's statement; "Whatever God made, we must consider blessed" (Ti-Jean and his Brothers, 139). At the time of the action of the play, Chantal's exploits have achieved legendary status. Only old Charlemagne recognises him and reminds Sonson of the stories about his madness. Popo laughs at his physical condition and wonders if life really holds any monsters since this one has been reduced so far. His levity is cut short by the appearance of a body in the rain-swollen stream nearby. It is the body of the white planter Regis, whom members of the group assume must have been murdered by Chantal.

Taking advantage of their fear, Chantal decides to play a macabre game. In a situation reminiscent of the trial-by-fool scene near the end of Brecht's The Caucasian Chalk Circle, the mad woodcutter decides to pass judgment on those who so readily condemn him. What they do not yet know is that he killed Regis in defending Moumou. He intervened just as the planter would have shot the deaf-mute for having stolen his silverware. Before beginning his interrogation, Chantal warns that he truth they claim to care about will not be as palatable as they believe. Threatened with the cutlass, Madeleine confesses her adultery. Pressed to declare the sentence on his wife Popo instead declares that in spite of his mistreatment of her, his love flawed as it is, will not permit him to condemn her now. Charlemagne has no undisclosed sin to confess. For years he has borne openly the guilt of having committed adultery with his brother's wife. He suffers too because he can no longer endure the hatred of a boy who could be his own son.

Satisfied that he has made his point about guilt and truth, Chantal ends his mock trial in acquittal. Ironically at that point, the deaf-mute, whose life he had saved, misinterprets Chantal's intentions and – believing that he is saving the entire group from a murder – stabs Chantal in the back. Mortally wounded, sensing Moumou's motivation, Chantal reinforces his point about the deceptive nature of life's appearance. "You see how a man can have a good meaning and do the wrong thing?" In this way layer, by layer, the play's complex meaning unfolds. The slayer who acted to save someone else becomes the victim of the one he saved.

The truth, of which so much is made in the dialogue, can never be fully disclosed. All but old Charlemagne desert him in his dying moments: and by leaving they never get to know the soul within Chantal. Asked if he needs a priest, Chantal answers in a way that indicated the unsuspected depths of love and beauty that lie buried under his offensive exterior.[66]

If one applies Derrida's "negative theology", his suspicion of the overt intention of the text and apply it to the theological assumptions of Malcochon, or the Six in the Rain, one might find some divergences from Hamner's neat assessment. In deconstructing the discourse of the text one finds more victims/slayers than Hamner's lone Chantal for a start. One not only confronts the hierarchical opposition of victim/slayer but intention/ action and reality/appearance. The first term of the opposition is the superior term, the second term the inferior term, thus 'victim' is the superior term, while 'slayer' the inferior term as is intention/action, 'intention' is the superior term while 'action' is the inferior, as is 'reality' the superior term, while appearance is the 'inferior' term.

In the victim/slayer opposition, while Chantal, the brute might have taken the white planter Regis' life, both are victims both have been slain,

Chantal by Moumou, the man whose life he saves; and Regis by Chantal in saving Moumou's life.

> *Well, friend. We in it now eh? A dead man in the rain face down in the mud and the wet leaves and an idiot with no tongue. Why I come down from the forest at all. . . Who will believe me? An old thief? A madman.*[67]

Thus the victim/slayer hierarchical opposition poses Chantal/ Moumou, Regis/Chantal equations. Chantal is thus both victim and slayer, he embodies no oppositions but embraces within his person both victim and slayer. Moumou, the would-be victim of Regis, and victim by birth, then becomes the slayer of Chantal. Who is this Mou-Mou? We know that he is a deaf-mute, he lives in a world of silence, he relies on his sense of sight to survive in the world, language is as dead and as meaningless to him as is the language of the text which dissembles by making of Chantal both victim and slayer, in obliterating the difference between the categories and makes of Moumou a victim/slayer also. This creates the deconstructionist's delight, the aporia, the gap in meaning and contributes to the negation, to the disruption of the first item. Language thus becomes a discredited tool and undermines the authority of the text.

Moumou is also a man without a tongue, who steals Regis' silver spoons and is saved from Regis' murderous wrath by Chantal who muses after. 'A dead man for a few silver spoons!' Regis thus becomes a would-be slayer, a victim of materialism. It is a betrayal of the spirit to be moved to murder by one's attachment to matter to consider Moumou's life so worthless, and these silver spoons so priceless, but it is the slayer Chantal who perceives the moral and ethical bankruptcy of the sacrifice! A dead man for 'a few silver spoons'. Certainly for Chantal whether the dead man were Moumou or Regis, it would still have been an unworthy exchange. Moumou the deaf is as precious as Regis the "white planter". Chantal of course reminds us of the most exalted victim and for him the victim/slayer opposition is God's son/ mankind – God's son is the victim and the slayer is mankind. Mankind, he insists, is a beast and God is a tolerant God who understands human frailties.

> *So what God means to say was "Thou should not kill",*
> *Knowing man will do it anyway, and the magistrate,*
> *The priest and so on, they did not understand that.*[68]

Thus Moumou is also a compassionate saviour, after all his act of murder, his turning against a friend is justified by his concern for the welfare of his fellowmen, whom he thinks are in danger. His instructive move towards the weeping wife, who denies Chantal's charge of adultery at first is very touching. Moumou's status as would-be victim, compassionate/slayer is curiously paralleled by victim/slayer; God-Son/mankind slayer. Does that make Moumou God's Son? And Victim/slayer, Chantal God's son also? Of course, but where does that leave Regis? Is he just a victim, without the saving grace of having compassion. This is certainly dethronement of the "king" Regis, the self-destruction of the rhetoric of the text. Regis is washed away by the flood, he becomes flotsam, he is the debris of the new dispensation, part of a wrecked order as he drifts out to sea. The authority of the white planter Regis, the king-pin of colonial society is destroyed as is the authority of the text.

> *A white man turning among loose water-lilies*
> *Leaves on his face and turning in the water*
> *Rolling in a muddy ditch going down to the Sea.*[69]

The hierarchical oppositions of intention/action conform to the theological definition of sin as missing the mark, as Chantal so aptly puts it.

> *You see how a man can have a*
> *Good meaning and do the wrong thing.*[70]

Intention is the superior term in this binary opposition while action is the inferior term. Intention fulfils the role of the ideal, the good meaning, while action does not correspond with this good intention. Yet inherent in positing intention/action as hierarchical oppositions is the contradiction that unless intention and action are congruent, the idealism inherent in "good intention" is negated by "doing the wrong thing". So that the characters who manifest a congruence between intention/action however despicable or negative are "superior" to those who "miss the mark". This negates any superiority in the first term "intention" as such. Characters who can be identified in the intention/action category are Charlemagne/Sonson, Madeleine/Popo, Chantal/Moumou. It is Charlemagne's good intention to help his nephew by warning him against his judgmental attitude with its concomitant feelings of hatred towards his uncle, for his adulterous past. The old man wishes to leave that past behind him, to start anew, but the nephew does not:

> *Remember how your brother kill his wife for you nastiness...*[71]

Charlemagne's reprimand of his nephew is no less pointed:

You have the same blood, the madness and the hatred. . .[72]

This indictment points to both concern and fear by Charlemagne, concern about his nephew's mental state and fear that like his brother, Sonson's father, he can become a murderer too. Is this ambivalence, this good intention, "missing the mark", in that it neither gives Son-Son a positive image of himself nor any help in moving beyond either father or uncle in consciousness? There is negation upon negation in the exercise. The nephew's actions of dragging up the past and embarrassing his uncle are consonant with his intentions, which are far from idealistic. He simply, lamely seeks to discomfort his uncle and nurse his grievances against him. So that the uncle movingly anticipates his future in a "good pitchpine coffin":

My own dry house, where no wind will come,
Where the rain cannot reach me, and I cannot hear
the thunder
A good pitchpine coffin. I cannot live in all this hatred.[73]

The real difference between the old man's intentions/action is not so much between his intention and his action but within his intention itself, for while he intends to initiate some change in the young man's behaviour by focusing on the negative links to his parents, he refuses to accept his own behaviour, in terms of his links with his brother the murderer, thus the meaning of the connection is lost to him as he unconsciously severs himself from the link with "blood", "madness", "hatred" and becomes self-righteous. He denies himself the compassion and love that ate his by right of his humanity, while the nephew in his consistency and congruence of intention/action appears more human, however unsavoury might be his personality, thus the suspicion that there is a gap between the intention of the language and the action of the play.

In the Madeleine/Popo opposition. Madeleine is identified with "intention" in the Intention/Action hierarchy, her dubious intention is to be punished for her wrong-doing albeit subconsciously. She seeks, ... demands to be "killed", but her actions do not match this high intention of expurgation; for she seeks no forgiveness, she is fiercely proud, and she taunts her husband, undermining his self-esteem while daring him to kill her. It is the gift of a cheap bottle of white rum, Malcochon, that serves as the catalyst for this marital struggle.

Is you who crazy! Well then leave me alone, or kill me then, kill me. Because a man
give me a bottle? But I not standing up in the white rain to talk nastiness with you.[74]

She calls him "coward", "hypocrite", "dog":

> *...Just like a dog. In front of me he give jokes, he can shame his wife in front of strangers. Look at the brave dog that putting his tail between his legs for a flash of lightning...*[75]

Popo the wronged husband thinks he loves his wife, but his love is so possessive, his pride so great that his wife fears his forgiveness more than she fears death, after confessing to her adultery she pleads,

> *Kill me, Chantal! Kill me! He cannot forgive*
> *I could never look in his face in my whole life again*
> *I cannot stand the shame of his forgiveness*
> *Because even his forgiveness is part of his pride*
> *What am I to him? What he think of me now?*
> *Don't ask him for mercy, because he will give it*
> *And boast about it always. Don't turn him into God!*[76]

Poor Madeleine's concept of God is as circumscribed as is her husband's concept of love. While she believes in a fearsome and judgmental God, he needs to be genuinely forgiving and humble. He alienates his wife from him by not accepting that he, like all men, is involved in this fall from grace. Yet the difference within his own good meaning/intention is not so much doing the wrong thing, as it is doing the right thing (loving) for the wrong reason, that is demanding of her perfection, which he quite rightly acknowledges he is incapable of:

> *I am a fool with ordinary sins.*
> *Jealousy is one, and love is mixed with jealousy.*
> *Jealousy is a disappointment Madeleine,*
> *That what we love is not perfect.*[77]

Both Madeleine and Popo "miss the mark" there is no congruence between their intention/action, they are equally culpable and palpably human.

The Chantal/Moumou pair, present the main contradictions in the Intention/Action binary oppositions. Chantal, the felon, the fearsome legend, the "madman of the forest", is certainly not a candidate for good intentions or idealism and yet it is Chantal who presents us with the most constructive example of sacrifice. It is his experience of "vicarious suffering" that catapults him into a position of exemplar of selfless love. He not only murders Regis in order to save Moumou from being murdered, but he is in turn murdered by Moumou who thinks his "saviour" is about to commit other murders. Moumou believes that he is now placed in the role of saviour, mistakenly of course. Both Chantal and Moumou's intentions are idealistic, both consider themselves saviours, but are saviours associated with murder rather than with love; with death rather than with life. Both the felon and the deaf-mute exhibit a congruence of behaviour, yet the deaf-mute can be partially excused for his actions, since without language he partially interprets the world – the felon with language interprets the threat to Moumou correctly – Yet the gift of language makes not an iota of difference in these two men's murderous reactions. Is the intention of language itself not congruent with its action, its rhetoric? The edifice of the discourse itself crumbles.

The reality/appearance binary opposition concedes the superior term to be reality and the inferior term to be appearance, the illusion. The characters fall into place almost naturally as representatives of these concepts. Madeleine/Popo, Charlemagne/Sonson and Chantal/Moumou.

Chantal's dangerous charade of hearing confessions from his fellow-travelers has the effect of removing the veil from the characters. Chantal has been moved to unearth the "truth" because of the insistence of everyone on knowing the truth. He says:

> ...From the time I here, I hear
> all four of you talking about the truth.
> Well, I will give you the truth and see what
> you can do with it.[78]

The reality is that Chantal disturbs the values of western culture, by stripping the veil of hypocrisy off the other 'good' citizens. He stands morally above the searchers of truth, who are quite incapable of facing up to this 'truth' which they seek. He is the symbol of the superior moral value of the truly honest self-accepting man. He is the voice of the anti-establishment text which questions the validity of the establishment's honesty in his search for truth. What is truth? Pilate asks Jesus. What is truth Chantal dares to ask his judges, those who cannot forgive his former life of a thief who have consigned him to the forest, a wandering old madman.

Madeleine of "the nice hair", the attractive wife of Popo, with all her taunting and teasing and challenging him to kill her, is really a lying adulterous woman, while Popo the long-suffering cukold who appears weak, lacking in self-respect and jealous, is in reality quite magnanimous when confronted with the truth of his wife's adultery. He says:

> *I love my wife, sir, and will be jealous of her*
> *Till the day she is dead, and if God take her*
> *And leave me in this earth, I will jealous of God*
> *What I saying is the truth. Don't cry, Madeleine*
> *You can cut my neck off, but that is the truth.*[79]

Charlemagne, the old man, is an adulterer, he is concerned about his nephew's hatred towards him. He even begs Chantal to kill him.

> *If you must kill somebody, kill me, old tiger!*
> *Kill me. I am tired. And today I know the truth,*
> *That this animal here who could be my own son*
> *Could be a serpent from the hatred he have for me.*[80]

He is the only one who stays with the dying Chantal. Yet he appears to be carping and insensitive toward his nephew's predicament, while the nephew who appears to be a victim of terrible circumstances, the loss of his parents, is in reality very self-righteous, judgmental and full of hatred, he indicts all women when he says:

> *They lie! They lie! On their death bed they will lie,*
> *They have mothers who take their secret to the grave.*
> *On their birth-bed they lie. My father was right.*[81]

One loses all sympathy with his fate when one realises the depth of his bitterness and unforgiveness.

Moumou's appearance is quite unprepossessing, he evokes sympathy as a deaf-mute, he appears as the "poor beast" ..."poor animal", he is the "mongoose", but despite this animal imagery, Moumou is in reality very human. His motive for murdering Chantal is the highest of human motives – to save others, Chantal who says of himself:

> *Oh, if only I wasn't so ugly, I could sin like a beautiful woman and nobody would*
> *hold it against me.*[82]

He who is referred to as:

> *This old man there with the broken teeth and the croak voice, with one crooked eye and*
> *marks on his face, this is Chantal the wood demon, that we was frighten of as children.*[83]

This "wood demon" Chantal seems to be in tune with the concept of the loving forgiving God of the New Testament. He is sure that his sins will be forgiven he believes that he has fixed that up with God already. His faith in God, in some principle of good is greater than many a priest whom he fears might go "crazy" listening to his sins. The appearance of the "ugly wood demon" does not match the reality of the forgiving, understanding Chantal who readily understands Moumou's mistake in striking him down.

He responds to the old man's assessment of Mou-mou as "a small dog" with the words:

with a good heart. He have a good heart.[84]

There is no rancour, no regret. The Moumou/Chantal concept of reality attests to the superiority of their characters but they are both murderers. Has language itself betrayed its purpose? Is Derrida right? There is always something that escapes since writing itself is a form of escape from any scheme designed to shut it down.

Said says of Derrida:

Derrida everywhere identifies with metaphysics and its hierarchies, the other half of which allows the detonation of writing in the very interior of the word, thus disrupting the entire given order and taking over the field.[85]

It is the "aporia", the hole left by the detonation of writing, the explosion of contradiction, where the text involuntarily betrays the tension between rhetoric and logic, between what it manifestly means to say and what it is nonetheless constrained to mean that creates of the text Malcochon or the Six in the Rain, the deconstructive delight that it is. Derrida's 'negative theology' and the theology of Malcochon complement each other.

Historical Plays

A S we leave unaccommodated man in the folk plays, we experience the traumas of colonized man as he seeks to experience himself in a historical context. Man is seen as he creatively comes to terms with slavery, colonization, uprootedness and displacement. He is seen in his search for freedom and for an identity while recognizing his otherness from his Imperial master. Walcott makes of these experiences two fascinating plays. *Henri Christophe* is a youthful play. The playwright confides that he was in search of ruins of a towering figure to exercise his precocious genius. He wanted to affirm that something noble was created in this New World in this Caribbean. Nothing was more noble than the establishment of the independent state of Hayti, made so by slaves. The other play is *The Last Carnival.* It examines the French Creole influence on culture in the island of Trinidad. As a mature writer, he uses the techniques of post-colonial literature, using a counter-discursive technique. This he does by a process of appropriation, abrogation and syncreticism. He extols the virtue of creolization.

There is an interesting correlation between the deconstructive approach to literary criticism and post-colonial theory. Derrida believed that deconstruction was a political practice, an attempt to dismantle the logic by which a particular system of thought, a political structure and social institutions maintain their force. The experience of the colonized was an experience which reinforced the political system, structure and social institutions of the colonizer by sheer dint of conquest. All that post-colonial literature strives to do is to deconstruct this imperial discourse which marginalized it. Post-colonial literary theory seeks to outline and delineate the themes of this literature. In accepting itself as "other", as outside of the master text, it is challenging the assumption of the binary opposition which class, caste, and culture assume. It has subverted the hegemony of the master text, while moving itself from margin to centre.

Both Henri Christophe and The Last Carnival fall into the category of post-colonial literature, and as such, they share certain characteristics of literature emerging from and affected by the imperial process from colonization to the present day. These literatures assert themselves by foregrounding the tension with the imperial centre and by emphasizing their differences from the imperial centre.[1] While in Henri Christophe the conflict which surrounds the power struggle is elemental, it is the violence of war, in the play The Last Carnival, the power struggle manifests itself in language. Yet, since cultures thrive in conflict, Henri Christophe, the play, is as much about military power as about linguistic power. Language becomes a medium through which a hierarchical structure of power is perpetuated and the medium through which conceptions of truth, order and reality become established.[2] Thus the signification of authority which writing represents is an attempt to wrest power from the dominant European culture.

Foucault's perception is that the history which bears and determines us has the form of war rather than that of a language, these are relations of power not relations of meaning. Language itself is seen as contradiction. This is interesting for the real reason that what is said and who says it constitute meaning over and above that of the sign:

> *Words, expressions, propositions, etc. . .change their meaning according to the position held by those who use them, which signifies that they find their meaning by reference to these positions.*[3]

The words of the colonizers have meanings which the colonized cannot appropriate with the same authority. Toussaint's words were precisely those of the Jacobins of the French revolution, yet had different resonances in imperial France. He after all was a former slave. Henri Christophe must be seen as the heir of C L R James' Black Jacobins.

Said observes that James' Black Jacobins

> *. . .bridges an important cultural and political gap between Caribbean, specifically Black history, on the one hand, and Caribbean history on the other. Yet it too is fed by more currents and flows in a wider stream than even its rich narrative may suggest.*[4]

These currents and flows also include the themes of Black inferiority from hierarchies of advanced to underdeveloped subject races. The unchallenged authority of the white race is buttressed by images, notions, quasi-scientific concepts about barbarism, primitivism and civilization. All these were given credibility through anthropology, Darwinism, Christianity,

Utilitarianism, idealism, racial theory, legal history, linguistics and the lore of intrepid travellers. What Said terms the lingua franca of men like Carlyle and Froude is a language that is global, comprehensive and with that vast social authority that is accessible to any racist imperialist; as such it is imbued with great power. Compare Froude's assessment of Independent Hayti with James' description of Toussaint in Black Jacobins.

Froude's dictum on Hayti almost eighty years after its Independence is revealing: "...that Hayti was the most ridiculous caricature of civilization in the whole world."[5] One notes the implication of the grotesque, the mimicry, the laughable attempts of people – and it is never decided for sure by Froude and his ilk that Black people were people – to pretend to be civilized, a thing he has never heard of in the entire world. This is the same Froude who observed that:

> ...*one or other of them occasionally rises in the legal or other profession, but there is no sign, not the slightest, that the generality of the race are improving either in intelligence or moral habits; all the evidence is the other way.*[6]

While J. J. Thomas' Froudacity is a fitting rejection of his assessment of black people and of the "negro-phobic political hobgoblin', James' description of Toussaint in the Black Jacobins shows the gulf between the view from the centre and that from the margins of empire. The view from the centre is, to put it kindly, a most jaundiced one, for it raises the question of whether mimicry/creativity negates intelligence, or whether they attest to very human qualities. James recognizes that the world of discourse inhabited by natives of the Caribbean is dependent on the West.

He states:

> ...*in the hour of danger Toussaint, uninstructed as he was, could find the language and accent of a Diderot, Rousseau and Raynel of Mirabeau, Robespierre and Danton. And in one respect he excelled them all. For even these masters of the spoken and written word, owing to the class complications of their society, too often had to pause, to hesitate, to qualify. Toussaint could defend the freedom of the blacks without reservation, and this gave to his declaration a strength and a single mindedness rare in the great documents of time. The French bourgeoisie could not understand it. Rivers of blood were to flow before they understood that, elevated as was his tone, Toussaint had written neither bombast nor rhetoric but simple and sober truth.*[7]

The French bourgeoisie could not understand the phenomenon of Toussaint, neither could Froude for they were locked into, and limited by a myth of white superiority and black inferiority which blinded them to the obvious, that there was nothing inferior about Toussaint's ability to internalize the truth of the universalist sentiments of European Enlightenment. Toussaint's flaw was in taking them as literal intentions rather than class and history-determined remarks of interest groups. The view from the centre is committed to its world construct and in Hayti's case, underestimates the opposition in the intellectual as well as the battlefield. James' vision of history and politics is linear, as Said states:

He saw the central pattern of politics and history in linear terms – from Du Bois to Fanon from Toussaint to Castro – and his basic metaphor is that of a voyage taken by ideas and people, those who were slaves and subservient classes could first become the immigrants and then the principal intellectuals of a diverse new society.[8]

It is in this 'story line', this narrative of James' that Walcott's Henri Christophe and The Last Carnival fit; these plays are the descendants of the Froude/Thomas/James imperial/colonial discourses. In Henri Christophe, when Brelle the catholic priest says:

We cannot answer vengeance with vengeance, because
As far as the eye can warn the incision instruct,
The cycle will never end. Blood flows
Where blood is uprooted...[9]

There is an essential contradiction in the language here, not simply because Brelle's assumptions about Dessalines preclude his understanding of such concepts, but more interestingly, Brelle is asking of Dessalines to behave in ways in which the dominant power which he represents never behaved, never with such rationality. Here is an attempt to stem the consequences of the brutality of slavery and imperialism by assuming the high moral/Christian ground of compassion, tolerance, forgiveness, 'turning the other cheek' and breaking the cycle of violence. Brelle assumes that his power over language is also his power over the ex-slave thereby ensuring his compliance.

Dessalines reminds us of the irrationality of the behaviour of priests like Brelle. While Dessalines might not have the 'power' nor the 'order' behind him, he represents a reality and a truth that is uncomfortable for Brelle:

While Jesuit fathers built presbyteries from slavery,
Swinging a nulling incense over wound-humped backs
Tired with the weight of Africa
Baptizing with a tongue in cheek...[10]

His speech too is a contradiction, it is not even presumed that what he says would have the same meaning for Brelle, that when he talks of 'brutality' as in 'wound-humped' backs it means the same as Brelle's 'blood is uprooted'. Dessalines is not only denying Brelle the privilege of his negation of him as a man, but he is opposing Brelle's use of language to indict the ex-slave's right to vengeance, by reminding him of the Jesuits' implication in the blood letting of slaves.

The Last Carnival demonstrates the intensity of the cultural struggle, the battleground on which imperialism's demise is predicated. Said suggests that:

> ...culture is a sort of theatre whose various political and ideological causes engage one another. Far from being a placid realm of Appollonian gentility, culture can even be a battleground on which causes expose themselves to the light of day and contend with one another.[11]

The forces of Imperial French culture and the Creole culture of Trinidad battle it out in this play. When French-Creole Victor says to British Agatha:

> You'll look around you and all you'll see is fiction
> Some colourful backwater of the Empire.[12]

One could not be further from the centre than that. Yet it is Victor who clings to his identification with the "centre", the "metropole", while Oswald, his brother is fixed on the "margin", the "backwater".

The true transformation takes place through Victor's heirs. The battle between the promoters of the "centre" and the proponents of the "margin" ends in stalemate. It is the heirs of the combatants – the transformers of this culture who win – they reject the dominant/marginal paternalistic discourse, the pseudo-conflict between periphery/centre, they jettison it all by embracing the syncretic, the hybrid, the Creole. Oswald's reaction to his brother dressed in the French Impressionist Watteau's costume, marks him as on the periphery, one from the "backwater' of Empire.

> And look, Monsieur Watteau himself! Victor, oh God. Carnival is carnival and art is art. And never shall the twain fucking meet. Two brothers, same family. Different temperament, but I don't think we should do this...[13]

There is nothing gentle about this battle. It ends in stalemate. It is the heirs, the inheritors who find a resolution to the conflict. Tony, Victor's son rejects the father, "that fraud", he calls him:

I despise the British. Except Aggie who's one of us. I hate the French, I detest anything French that shows in me, and I suppose, although I love my father I detested him. He made us cherish taste, and it was the wrong taste for this country and that makes us useless.[14]

Yet it is this son who transmutes and transforms his "Frenchness", his "taste", his art into costumes for Carnival, into something indigenous. His sister Clodia, whose French is "horrible" and who is proud to be a Trinidadian, thus "centering" her life in Trinidad, transforming her status of "backwater" inhabitant, says:

And I can't stand all you intellectuals who keep changing your mind and your skin, because maybe my father was no great shakes as an artist, but he wasn't no damn lizard to change when colours changed. He loved this place, and what hurt him was how he couldn't express that love of it beautifully enough, but Goddamn it, if he didn't make anything great, Goddamn it, he made me. . .[15]

This proud product of hybridity, of creolization serves as a metaphor for the transformative power of post-colonial literature, moving it from the margins, the "backwater of Empire" to the centre of world literatures and dethroning the hegemony of the Imperial canons.

HENRI CHRISTOPHE

VASTEY:	*In death Henri, the bone is anonymous;*
	Complexions only grin above the skeleton;
	Under the grass the dust is an anthology of creeds and skins
	Who can tell what that skull was?
	Was it for that we quarrelled?
CHRISTOPHE:	*Yes, fool, for that Hayti bled,*
	And spilled the valuable aristocratic blood
	To build those citadels for this complexion
	Signed by the sun
	Yes, for that we killed, because some were black,
	And some were spat on.
	For that I overturned the horn of plenty.
	And harvest grey hairs and calumny.
	It is I who history gave the voice to shout anarchy
	Against the king. I made this king they hate,
	Shaped out of slaves. . .
	What have I done, what have I done, Vastey, to deserve all this?[16]

Said observes that Imperialism's most paradoxical gift was to allow people to believe that they were mainly, exclusively white or black, or Western or Oriental, and that just as human beings make their own history, they also make their own cultures and ethnic identities. [17] It is the post-imperial writers particularly of the so-called "Third World" who bear their past within them, as scars of humiliating wounds, who seek to re-interpret their history and to re-define their culture. Liberation from this past becomes an intellectual mission, and:

> . . .*the best of them will choose the focus on rhetoric, ideas and language rather than history, preferring to analyze and/or use the verbal symptoms of power rather than its brute exercise, its intellectual methods, rather than its morality – to deconstruct rather than destroy.*[18]

It is not by accident that Walcott who was interested in drama, wanted to find an indigenous hero to write about in the high-flown dramatic style of the Jacobean plays which he as a school boy had been reading. Nor are the quotations from Shakespeare which precede Part I and Part II of this play arbitrary. These serve to remind the writer of his objective and to reinforce his intention to "beat the Imperialists at their own game." Yet the remarkable emphasis on "complexion" or "black" in the play speaks directly to the struggle of the post-colonial writer to dispel, to examine and to refute the "lingua franca' of the Imperialists' assumptions about 'natives', the Froudes and the Carlyles who spoke so eloquently on the "nigger question". On the other hand, the writer presents himself, as do James' Black Jacobins, as emissaries to Western culture, representing a political freedom and accomplishment as yet "unfulfilled, blocked, postponed".[19]

Henri Christophe elaborates the Haytian Revolution which was fired by the French Revolution's Jacobin slogans of "liberty, equality and fraternity", taken up by and internalized in the slave leaders. It traces the trials of the Republic from the death of Toussaint, to the rise of Dessalines, his demise through the rise and fall of Henri Christophe. Toussaint was betrayed by the French and lured to his death in France, he was a victim of his naive belief in the integrity of the Imperialists who could only defeat him through subterfuge. He is immortalized by the poet in these words spoken by Christophe:

Toussaint:
I cannot list his braveries, I can only tell
things that the memory shudders to remember,
Hurt by its love. He broke three nations,

> *He disrupted intrigues, curbed civil wars;*
> *He was no hammock General directing fools*
> *Into a cannon's yawn, he rode to wars with you,*
> *He held his generals, although they were refractory*
> *Like those who triumphed in Troy after*
> *The duplicity of the horse —*
> *Scylla, Maurepas, Dessalines, Petion;*
> *He forded rivers, a furious forager.*
> *But now they tell me he is made limp in spirit,*
> *Crucified in a winter's stubborn nails,*
> *An old man dancing on a stick of time, all skin and groan*
> *Wearing respectability to rags, died,*
> *Coughing on a stone floor.*
> *All this because a man was black.*
> *But we must triumph under that winter death*
> *I will perform the rites of spring, if*
> *you will let me, or let Dessalines...*
> *We need more than a wavering sceptre in this twilight.*
> *Slavery must never hold us again, not while*
> *I live.*[20]

Here is a brilliant display of language as power. The language used to celebrate the life of Toussaint reflects the ease with which the native manipulates the dominant code. It displays itself as an intimate participant in Western culture, it is subversive in intent. The dying Toussaint "coughing on a stone floor" will not be forgotten. Victim as he is of the power of superior arms and strategies. His life will be remembered because of the power of language, albeit a borrowed one.

The drama shifts from the death of Toussaint to the imminent rise of Dessalines. The essential difference between the two protagonists, Dessalines and Christophe, is that while Dessalines had no problem with his self-esteem and self worth, and was single-minded about what he perceived as the real issue, Christophe is brooding, infected with the horror of self-hatred, paralyzed by internalizing racism's shafts. He is paranoid in the castle of his burnished skin. He is consumed by the power of the aristocracy of the skin game. Compare Dessalines' speech with Christophe's, Dessalines thought that slavery was a temporary aberration, that they had fought for their freedom and won it, and now he would avenge himself on the perpetrators of this foul deed.

We have beaten the French, splintered
Napoleon's indestructibles, fever has furrowed them
Sickness scythed them in harvest. . .
Think, gentlemen, a black nobility, the white flower destroyed.[21]

This speech opens up the gap between the language which expresses conquest, raw power and the emergence of a black nobility at the expense of the white flower. Yet the white flower is not destroyed since it lives in Dessalines' choice of language, his appropriation of the particular means of signification. Christophe, on the other hand, chides Brelle thus:

O shut that hypocrite heart
Gabbling of love while you mock our complexions.[22]

It would be his castles, citadels and cathedrals which would function as the objective correlative of his paranoia, cloaking him in majesty, blinding others not himself to the colour of his skin. The most lyrical lines of the play empower this obsession.

On that blue smoking citadel
That hides the sun until its zenith by its height
I will build a fort
Made out of stone, as befits a soldier
Magnificent in marble, a king's comfort.[23]

OR

Caprices! Who talk of caprices?
I will exhaust this country into riches. Have you seen
The contagion of blight settling on the times like apathy
On our stalks? I will build any cathedral in a month,
then break or build this kingdom
Look, look up that hill. . .[24]

OR

Let us build white-pointed citadels,
Crusted with white perfections over
This epilogue of Eden, a prosperous Hayti,
My kingdom where I a king rule
Mine, mine, Vastey! Once slave,
Then after that Napoleon can envy
With the Antilles mine, the whole archipelago overturning

Cauldrons of history and violence on their master's hands
The slaves, the kings, the blacks, the brave.[25]

OR

I shall build chateaux
That shall obstruct the strongest season
So high the hawk shall giddy in its gyre
Before it settles on the carved turrets.[26]

Of course the security and transcendence Christophe seeks do not simply elude him but paralyze and cramp his style. For this power game is not won on the terms of the dominant power, it is not won by imitating their structures, it is won by deconstructing them. It is won by deconstructing the Imperial discourse and exposing the gaps, the "aporias" of the race-constructed, power-tower, it is a battle which can be won neither through Dessalines-like revenge nor self-hatred but through reconstruction and transformation of the culture and history in the process of accepting "white bread" – recognize one's inextricable involvement in Western culture, that after all is the meaning of the Black Jacobins, it is an irreversible collision of cultures. Archbishop Brelle points the way when he rebukes Christophe thus:

They are my people too, king.
And they are black;
Spiritual power has never made me despotic;
As temporal power has made you insane, neurotic,
What kind of perverse kindness is it that denies them white bread,
But will not let a friend call them black? [27]
Christophe replies:
You say it again,
Priest, I am tired of your complexion,
I have had too much to do with this
Besides you talk to no slave.[28]

Tired Christophe might be, but it is imperative that he transforms his tiredness in creative ways or perish. One must confront and acknowledge the causes of Christophe's "tiredness" with Brelle, with white complexions. One must confront and acknowledge the power of the "white world". The power of their word to circumscribe and delimit the colonized potential of the people. Froude's barley concealed distaste of Hayti is acknowledged thus:

I stayed no longer than the ship's business detained the captain, and I breathed more freely when I had left that miserable cross-birth of ferocity and philanthropic sentiment. No one can foretell the future fate of the black republic, but the present order of things cannot last in an island so close under the American.[29]

Froude seems to be holding his breath while trying to beat a hasty retreat from what seems to him to be an offensive odour, the effect of the "cross birth" of ferocity and philanthropic sentiment. What or where is the "philanthropic sentiment" to which he refers? One understands the "ferocity" as a code word for African descendants. Is Froude implying that Hayti became an independent black republic because of the humanity and goodwill of white men? Or are the "philanthropic sentiments" the Jacobin slogans of "liberty, equality and fraternity"? Whatever the interpretation, Froude disdains to give any credit to the Toussaints, Dessalines and Christophes for creating an Independent Republic. He only acknowledges "ferocity" as their contribution. He further states that:

> *Liberty in Hayti had been followed by a massacre of the French inhabitants and the French settlers had done no worse than we had done to deserve the ill will of their slaves.*[30]

Faint praise from Froude, that the French and the English are either just as good or as just as bad colonisers, but what a fate the poor French receive at the hands of the Haytians! It is the view from the margins rather than the view from the centre which Henri Christophe, the play addresses. Essentially it is the rise and fall of Christophe which is dramatised. Christophe is seen in his full humanity and vulnerability, his patriotism, his ambitions and his disillusionment, and finally his death. Yet nothing Froude says opens the curtain or sheds light on this human being.

Scylla speaks in the "lingua franca" of Froude as the news of Toussaint's death by betrayal is discussed in the context of a Hayti that is seen as "rudderless":

> *The peasants have identified with idleness;*
> *The fallow fields cropless, the old plantations;*
> *Plaine du Nord, Morne Rouge, Quartier Morin*
> *Are like grass windows, unweeded, growing thorns*
> *And bristles, dry seeds on a parching wind*
> *We do not seem to be able to drive them back to work;*
> *They speak of slavery murmur against measures*
> *Strict, but satisfactory to the able administrator.*[31]

The myth of the lazy, idle, peasant/slave, who needs to be made to work is given credence, while "they speak of slavery" is euphemistic. These statements do not betray the reality of that burden. Brelle too, recognizes the difficulty of the civilizing mission, how easy it is for the natives to revert to primitive practices.

The ancient cults are growing like an unweeded garden over
Our pruned labours.[32]

Dessalines, unlike Scylla and Brelle, ascribes intention and deliberation to the people, he speaks to them as determinants of their fate, circumscribed as this is, rather than as stereotypes

...if these men will not work
Since we have their good in our intentions
We will punish them like a stern father.[33]

It takes the marginalized Dessalines to affirm the humanity of the peasants, as he reflects on his perception of the "founders" of the country:

- the Big Whites
Wild geese that, adopting a finer climate, assume
The white divinity of the swan; and all their brothers
A babble of shopkeepers, murderers, dispossessed.
You say they founded this country. What did they found?
Bastardhoods whose existences they denied, privileges pruned,
Cruelties devised to adorn an indolent minute
While Jesuit fathers built presbyteries from slavery
Swinging anulling incense over wound-humped backs
Tired with the weight of Africa
Baptising with a tongue in cheek...[34]

He sees through the illusion with which the whites clothe the reality of their rapaciousness and cruelty, they "assume the white divinity of the swan". This assumption allows them the freedom to devise cruelties like slavery. This illusion is part of the religion which can swing anulling incense on wounded backs, it wipes out and makes "innocent" their cruelties – the exploitative nature of capitalism and slavery; the greed and immorality are all expiated by the church. Its ambivalent attitude to the slave is revealed in the weight/Baptising opposition of the African dilemma. The white man's burden, and the uncertainty of the status of the African. Is he human, does he have a soul to be saved through baptism? Let us "tongue in cheek" assume that he has. Dessalines' strength is in his honesty with himself and his honest assessment of the whites. He sees himself as a human being who has experienced pain, hurt and humiliation and who will ruthlessly avenge himself on those who have caused it. He has no scruples about removing those who stand in the way of his ambitions black or white.

> *White men are here; for every scar (baring his tunic)*
> *How on my unforgiving stomach, I'll murder children,*
> *I'll riot, I have not grown lunatic, I'll do it, I'll do it.*
> *You think I am not aware of your intrigues,*
> *Mulattoes and whites, Brelle and Petion;*
> *I am asking. Argue with history.*
> *Ask history and the white cruelties*
> *Who broke Boukman, Ogé Chevannes; ask Rochambeau*
> *If you will not comply, I'll go.*[35]

There is no denying for Dessalines the therapy of revenge:

> *No Henri, this is politics*
> *I cannot wear, Christ-like an albatross*
> *Around my neck; the wounds in my sides*
> *Were dug by innocent white hands, a king*
> *makes them pay for it.*[36]

Dessalines' curious representation of himself as a sovereign human being who has the right to revenge, also recognizes the destructiveness of his obsession. It is limiting to justify his humanity on the grounds of a negative reaction to racial hatred/slavery.

> *I carried a passage, rigorous as a dolphin*
> *Through the red fun. Oh, three wars cannot size*
> *Yesterday's horror.*
> *And yet I find no purpose for this fighting*
> *Have I gone mad after long war?*
> *Does murder grow like habit in the mind, infection*
> *In the fingers and the skull?*
> *Henri, I am mad. . .*[37]

The real tension of the play is sustained between the creativity and the power of the language and the sterility and destructive nature of revenge and self-hatred. It is thus through the hierarchical oppositions of creativity/language versus sterility/racist power relations, that the discourse is deconstructed. The real triumph of the play Henri Christophe is not the demise of the "kings" but the majesty of the language. Dessalines ironically voices the view from the "centre" when he says:

> You mock my colour
> You cannot think a black king real.[38]

This is said to Christophe who in consistent Christophe contemplation of colour states:

> I am not as ruddy as you.[39]

Ruddy! One wonders where will this all end, a real rainbow of colours has Christophe presented to us. Yet one should not digress. The triumph of the play lies in the "power" of the language. W. H. New notes:

> A characteristic of dominated literatures is an inevitable tendency towards subversion, and a study of the subversive strategies employed by post-colonial writers would reveal both the configurations of domination and imaginative and creative responses to the condition.[40]

The writer's use of techniques and devices of metropolitan scholarship used in original and creative ways, transforms the literature of the Caribbean, and at the same time moves it from the periphery of world literatures to the centre. Jacobean cadences blend with Creole care in some memorable lines spoken by the "kings" Dessalines and Christophe and their protagonist. Petion's insight into Dessalines' character is revealed in an extended metaphor of "dressing" as deception, as vaulting ambition's camouflage.

> Dressing in the inner room
> Preparing to be valedictory
> To this peace that holds its breath, to hear
> What happened to Toussaint.
> Today a ship arrived from France;
> Anchoring in the roads, she looked sullen;
> Fearing the worst, Dessalines would look decorous
> To suit the occasion. But if he really dressed his hope
> It would wear black; he would like Toussaint dead.
> This country that stretched, crowing to greet
> The sun of history rising, will have its throat cut;
> That's the truth.[41]

This is a precocious youth's perfecting of a style which does not "dress" his ambition to be the best writer he could be. Vastey's character is superbly drawn as the Machiavellian politician who pours poison into the ambitious Christophe's ear. He knows exactly what he would like to hear:

> *Dessalines is dangerous. Restless rulers;*
> *Dream to their pillows of personal power*
> *Now that Toussaint's dead, the choice is open*
> *To the strong man.*[42]

AND

> *My personal advice is. In your talk*
> *Do not be too smooth, show your discontent*
> *At being brushed off the chess board of history*
> *But play the pieces on the board with duplicity*
> *Until you are king of the hand of history.*[43]

As Christophe's magic works, he is easily convinced of his destiny to be king. The playwright's magic also works as he stakes his claim Anancy-like to dominance, to kingship. "A king flows in me." He is confident of his powers. His magic is his command of the master style, the Imperial language. Judging his own performance he will not countenance murder, he will not countenance the killing off of the very language, culture and institutions which inform his competence. In a king's eye this will be failure. Thus the Creole intention is specific, appropriate the language, make it as powerful as it can be by incorporating the wit, the rhythm of the Caribbean with the linguistic competence of the master trope.

Christophe is no Dessalines, he has no intention of destroying him – yet:

> *A king flows in me*
> *You have seen me command*
> *Cruel and lovingly when I burned Le cap,*
> *Rochambeau realmless, hurried to France.*
> *I judge my conduct*
> *In a king's eye, and find this failure.*[44]

His ambition will not countenance murder; this is "his failure", but it won't be long before he will be convinced about the correctness of this action. He becomes the defender of democracy and movingly accuses Dessalines of autocratic behaviour and its consequences:

I consider the articles expressed
In your constitution and I find
Hidden in your assembly's salad of words, dressed
In a kind of poison to any freedom
An evidence of autocracy
You have decided to assume a monarchy
Before Toussaint's breath faded from the glass of history
You consulted a clique, only a class
With twisted personal interests at its mind's end
In this rule there is an end
Of democracy, only a long exploitation
And a bitter harvest, an expiration
Of the breath of decency, financial depression
And I was never asked to give my impression.[45]

Here, one sees the counter-discursive technique at work as a strategy. Any autocratic assumption of power, whether of political power or an assumption of the hegemony of European literature is simply undemocratic. Like Christophe, no one ever enquired of the playwright what his impression is about all these matters. Since he was never consulted he will none the same represent his own interests, his own constituency and like Christophe contemplate the awesome burden of kingship of dominance, of sovereignty of style – of a careful passion to create something new.

Such a range of weighty topics is discussed and explored from the fringe of Empire! It is J. J. Thomas all over again refuting Froudacity, that denigrating document on West Indians. As Christophe contemplates the awesome burdens of kingship he ruminates on his fate and compares it with that of Dessalines:

I am tired of many things
Chief, living. This ephemeral gesture
Of a greying hero, with murders for his memory
I think, this is the tiredness
That threatened Dessalines before he died
Leave us, go home.[46]

How much like Macbeth he has become, the remorse of conscience he experiences is difficult to live with:

I had no comfort, what I wanted
Was memory which no worm bites, this summer flesh

Wrapped in comfort around the arctic bone
Will crumble like my work. You understand,
white man
This nigger search for fame
Dragged like a meteor across my black rule.[47]

Too late does Christophe realise that "worm bites". The rot at the heart
of the apple of temptation, cannot be forgotten. The temptations to which
one succumbs would not go away. Murder is difficult to live with. There are
always other ambitious politicians impatient to begin the cycle of violence
once more. Christophe will not give Petion the satisfaction of murdering
him. He kills himself, before he dies, he speaks his epitaph. It is a king's
view of history

I am not without pity, but pity comes
tardily and fits
Raggedly around my crimes. Besides I think,
In honesty, I am rather sorry
For myself that all those things I did
I cannot ripen compunction by rosaries
Or pray to Damballa or broken gods
History, breaking the stalk she grew herself
Kills us like flies, wings torn, held up to light.
Burning biographies like rubbish.
Skull, when your smile wore flesh around its teeth
Time like a pulse was knocking in the eyelid
The worm was mining in the bone for metal
What shall I leave?
I am alone. . .This anonymous skull?
What shall I. . .? A half-charred name"
No. A king's memory or oblivion
Tell Petion I leave him this dark monarchy
The graves of children, and years of silence. . .
And after that. . .
Oblivion and silence.[48]

What is the legacy of Christophe? A king's memory or oblivion? The
playwright proves that this legacy is not oblivion. Like Christophe, he must
destroy in himself the urge to live a life of imitating the master style. One
notes the playwright's Jacobean style. He must destroy the urge to consent to

the hegemony of the canonical works, or to display the uncertain acquisition of such a style. Thus, in working his craft in this youthful experiment he kills off his desire to perpetuate this mimicry. The inheritors of the imperial language, those whom "she grew herself" those who suffered cultural denigration and who historically accepted the power of the authority of the language must resist the murderous, stifling, destructive power of imitation and employ instead the techniques of appropriation, hybridity and syncreticity. In order to fly towards the light, to the centre, to be genuinely creative they must use the subversive power of the master style but they must delve beneath the surface, beneath the power structure to do so. It is the subterranean worm mining in the bone for the metal which will unearth the spirit of unaccommodated man, the colonial experience, the use of national language, the rhythms of the people. All these must be mined to produce the literature which breaks the silence and resounds throughout the world, moving it from oblivion to centre stage.

CULTURAL TRANSFORMATION, HISTORICAL PERSPECTIVES AND THE MOVEMENT FROM "BACKWATER" TO CENTRE STAGE: JUMPING IN *THE LAST CARNIVAL*

The Last Carnival attempts an examination of the historical process which takes Trinidad from crown colony to independent nation; it can be seen as an interrogation of Imperial culture. It is also a counter-discursive play about relocating the cultural centre from the periphery, from a perceived "backwater" of Empire, to its rightful central position in the Caribbean.

Trinidadian J. J. Thomas in his book Froudacity, a response to Anthony James Froude's The English in the West Indies, notes that contrary to Froude's depiction of the "so happy, so sleek and contented peasantry" that:

> *Any respectable, well-informed inhabitant of Trinidad who happened not to be an official "bird of passage" might on our author's honest inquiry, have informed him that Trinidad is the land of chronic agitation for Reform. Mr. Froude might also have been informed that, even forty-five years ago, that is in 1843, an elective constitution with all the electoral districts duly marked out, was formulated and transmitted by the leading inhabitants of Trinidad to the then secretary of state for the colonies.*[49]

Thomas went on to say that these self same Negroes were active "improvers and embellishers" of that very soil of Trinidad. It is this creative endeavour of improving and embellishing European culture that engages Walcott and which leads him to the formulation of the concept of "creolization" and the centrality of the culture of the Caribbean. One of the fascinating observations which one can make about this broadside of J. J. Thomas' to Froude is that he disidentifies with the stereotyping of Froude and transforms what would ordinarily have been an Imperialist, one sided, linguistic canon-attack into a linguistic triumph for Thomas and all natives who have been so vilified. Thomas attained his power through the 'word', the English word. Foucault maintains that:

> *The discourse of the post-colonial is therefore grounded on a struggle for power that power focussed in the control of the metropolitan language.*[50]

Post colonial literature in Trinidad and the Caribbean was fathered by men like J. J. Thomas and C. L. R. James, Derek Walcott bears a filial relationship to them.. In discussing the strategy of disidentification in response to the "lingua franca" of Imperialism, as an aspect of post-colonial literature, Pecheur promulgates different modalities, the third modality he claims recognizes the dominant ideology as inescapable, but transformable through disidentification. One would witness this phenomenon in The Last Carnival where the character Oswald contrasts with his brother Victor. We note a hierarchical opposition of identification/disidentification in the Victor/Oswald sibling relationship. Victor is the Francophile, while Oswald is the earthy Trinidadian. Said's observation that the paradox of Empire which brought so many cultures together should leave its subjects with the belief that people were mainly or exclusively white or black, Western or Oriental is true not only of the play Henri Christophe but of In an Fine Castle, the precursor of The Last Carnival.

In a Fine Castle is reworked and transformed into The Last Carnival precisely because of the limitations imposed on it by privileging and identifying with negative stereotypes based on skin colour. It was doomed to failure. A deconstruction of the "fine castle" opened up the aporias which undermined it. The Last Carnival on the other hand, foregrounds cultural transformation, subsumes the colour question and resolves the battle of Imperial cultural dominance through appropriation and abrogation.

The struggle in Fine Castle is between the old colonial society and militant black nationalism. Black nationalism represents the impulse to deny that anything beneficial came out of the old colonial society. It seeks to privilege the African experience, and the African world view (a view which few colonials believed existed). The playwright's view is clear. He insists that Caribbean people stop exploiting an idea of Africa out of both the wrong kind of pride and the wrong kind of heroic idealism – historical sentimentality he calls it. He insists that the fact of slavery must be taken without bitterness since this could lead to the fatality of thinking in terms of revenge.[51]

This could only lead to the struggle for power over truth, the truth of the immense benefits, which the colonial experience conferred especially the acquisition of the Imperial language.

The Last Carnival meets the criterion for truth, the truth of the counter-discursive power of the text, the truth of freedom to create over the sterility of limitation. It is a transformative work which employs post-colonial techniques of syncreticity, hybridity, appropriation and abrogation.

The struggle for power over truth in some sense mimics the metropolitan impulse of dominance which post-colonial critics such as Homi Babha have sought to address. Only by stressing the way in which the text transforms the societies and institutions within which it functions (its transformative work) can such a mimicry be avoided and replaced by a theory and practice which embrace difference and absence as material signs of power rather than negation of freedom, not subjugation of creativity, not liberations.[52]

The Last Carnival is firmly based on the embrace of difference and absence as signs of power rather than negation. The main character Brown of Fine Castle, is neither black not white. Walcott uses him symbolically not only to portray a neutralist, balanced rational stance but to illustrate the conflict between the old colonial society and militant black nationalism. His girlfriend Shelly represents the latter, while his brief flirtation with Clodia de la Fontaine represents the former. He gains entry to the castle of the de la Fontaine family as a reporter. The entry to the castle by the reporter is symbolic of the role of the writer or cultural intellectual, to show not simply how all "representations are constructed, for what purpose by whom and with what components"[53] but to reject the politics of identity as given.

In the old colonial society as symbolised by Clodia, there is arrogance and prejudice but also fear and exhaustion. It is clear that that society is rapidly dying. Clodia confesses a desire for martyrdom as expiation for the sins of the past. She has resigned her crown as carnival Queen in favour of a black girl. Brown also finds arrogance, intolerance and a vicious disregard even for the feelings of long standing friendship in the black militants' strike committee. In Act Two Brown finds himself alone having chosen to relinquish his ties with Clodia and preferring noncommitment rather than blind allegiance to a cause such as Shelly demands. Brown thus rejects the limitations of Black nationalism while not yet embracing difference and absence.

Two minor characters serve important functions, George, the de la Fontaine's lifelong servant is unmoved by Brown's gibes about his servility, his dignified silence deflects and defeats Brown's insensitivity, from him Brown learns the power of restraint. The playwright is here examining the strategy which would highlight one of the key themes of post-colonial literature, appropriation. What is the nature of the master/servant relationship as it relates to literary style? It reminds one of Walcott's poem, "Another Life" in which he says:

> *I had entered the house of literature as a houseboy*
> *filched as the slum child stole,*
> *as the young slave appropriated*
> *those heirlooms temptingly left*
> *with the Victorian homilies of Noli tangere.*[54]

Brown learns the power of restraint. He understands George's servility and dignified silence, as a strategy. One must serve one's apprenticeship in the master's house before understanding what could be appropriated or abrogated. What would serve one's style as one weaves one's cultural experience into the master's style, the master's language.

Elizabeth Prince, white wife of a black militant leader wastefully sacrifices her life in order not to embarrass her husband. Finding herself ostracized by her former friends she commits suicide, dying with her (unknown to her husband) is the unborn child that was to have been the fruit of the marriage. The allegorical nature of this play places it squarely in the category of post-colonial literature. Here one notes the self-inflicted death of the hegemony of the Imperial canon, since without the marriage of post-colonial literature and its unborn potential as the unborn child suggests, it is truly doomed. Without the techniques of appropriation and hybridity the potential of the old literature cannot be released. The unborn child motif reminds one of the Bolom in Ti-Jean, crying out for life – new, vibrant life. Without the syncreticism there is the moribund and the sterile.

The entry of the French into Trinidad is described by Eric Williams in his History of the People of Trinidad and Tobago thus:

> *Africa had been brought in by Spain into Trinidad and the West Indies as the solution*
> *of the labour problem. France was now brought into Trinidad as the solution of the*
> *problem of white management. A French planter from Grenada, Roume de St Laurent,*
> *visited Trinidad and submitted a memorandum to the King of France on March 20,*
> *1777. The result of this memorandum was to transform a backward Amerindian*
> *colony governed by Spain into a Spanish colony run by Frenchmen.*[55]

The essence of Roume de St Laurent's plan was to transfer as many planters as possible and their African slaves from the French islands of Martinique, Guadeloupe, Dominica, St Lucia, St Vincent and Grenada, since they had suffered from a variety of hardships, hurricanes, ants which destroyed the sugar crop, bankruptcy, debts, the low price of coffee and soil exhaustion. The Spanish Governor at the time, Chacon while bowing to the Spanish government's acceptance of the proposals of Roume de St Laurent, foresaw problems from the invasion of "foreign immigrants". The French Revolution was at its heights throughout all the West Indies and Chacon warned the Prince de la Paz of the possible consequences.

The tri-colour cockade which they worship as a symbol of liberty was displayed by many of these slaves and they persuaded their comrades to follow their example. This caused me to despatch several parties to the country to suppress right at the beginning such disorder, which is one of the most terrible in these colonies where slavery is the basis of agriculture...

The contact which our people of colour and our Negro slaves have had with the French and Republicans have made them think of liberty and equality and the first spark will light the whole colony into a blaze.

The English are attacking the French islands and as many of the Republicans as can escape fly to the shores of Trinidad where there is no force to prevent them settling. The greater part are Mulattoes and Negros which increases in consequence our numbers, and infuses them with the same ideas and desires and makes the danger of a rising more imminent each day.[56]

Chacon's fears were well-founded, the rapidity with which the colony of Trinidad had been peopled and extended, together with the contending Imperial conflict of interests precipitated the British capture of Trinidad from the Spaniard in 1797 when Britain and Spain were at war. After 300 years of Spanish rule and more recent French migration, Trinidad passed without a shot being fired into British hands.

The Last Carnival tries to show this system of relationship and distil this history almost two hundred years after the takeover by the British. The play covers the pre- independence years of 1948-1962 in Act I; 1970 in Act II. Clodia gives her version of the construct of the "castle" in which she, as a descendant of the French lives. It underscores the structure of the "delusion" that is Imperialism, the sense in which relationships have a history and structure which must be examined, and reconstructed as well as deconstructed to arrive at a transformation.

This castle. You want to know this castle's history?
It was built on cocoa. My great-grandfather bought it
Stone by imported stone, all the way from France;
He had delusions about aristocracy. Bought the title.
We're a faint, bastard branch of some damned duke,
Which justifies the "de" in De la Fontaine,
It's an imitation, a stone fantasy,
But don't tell that to Miss Willett, she'd deny it.[57]

Like the carnival which the French introduced to Trinidad, the illusion and fantasy of power and control which Imperialism represents can be unmasked. Imitation is not the way, mimicking the metropole culturally is futile. Transforming it is imperative. This is the message of The Last Carnival. Carnival is a celebration of Latin culture with its masquerades and balls. It was also rooted in fantasy, mainly sexual fantasy, a grand bacchanal which ended on Shrove Tuesday.

Carnival was a curious and contradictory mixture of reality and illusion. Reality because the racial and economic divisions of society were clearly demarcated and affirmed; all freed men stood together against the slaves (remember the season opened with the Christmas martial law) and although white and coloured were carefully segregated, they symbolically linked arms by sharing the festival as a collective.[58]

The word sharing is significant, slaves and freemen share this seminal Trinidad cultural art form, the secret of its modern day success. The slaves eventually took it over and stamped it indelibly as theirs. Carnival has become a symbol of freedom for the broad masses of people of Trinidad and Tobago, it has become a focal point for the elaboration of cultural retentions in music, dance, costume and ritual. While carnival began as a celebration of Latin culture, a moment of sexual fantasy, a grand bacchanal when different races and classes were as one, it became after the Emancipation of the slaves in 1833 an expression of rage and defiance. In its masks it caricatured the "prissy" masquerading of the French. It was a subversive actuality which tended to undermine the authority of the former masters, while the former slaves appropriated it by including in its expression African dances. Even today carnival always includes a band either of Zulu warriors or Kings of Africa. Thus it became hybridized as it expressed resistance and dissent from the establishment. In the same manner, The Last Carnival employs the techniques of abrogation and appropriation as literature which challenges the master text.

Carnival is transformed annually into something fresh and new. Calypso, an important component of carnival, employs in its lyrics rich puns, metaphors, wit and verbal play; the rhythm is pulsating and compelling. Some claim that calypso is very much a part of the African tradition of praise songs and songs composed for all occasions.

Robert Hamner observes in his book Derek Walcott:

> The culture in which Walcott grew to manhood was like the area's calypso, derived from a variety of sources. When he envisioned himself and his role as an artist, he took this basic duality into account. 'I am a kind of split writer. . .the mimetic, the narrative and dance element is strong on one side and the literary, the classical tradition is strong on the other.' Furthermore, he continues on the same subject, our most tragic folk songs and our most self-critical calypsos have a driving life-asserting force. Combine that in our literature with a long experience of classical forms and you're bound to have something exhilarating. By 1970 when he was recoding these ideas, he felt that his acting company had achieved a significant fusion of styles, a powerful physical expression combined with classic discipline.[59]

It is this fusion of styles, the syncreticity of styles if you will which is the essence of Walcott's theory of creolisation. He chooses to focus on rhetoric, ideas and language rather than history per se. He prefers to analyse the verbal symptoms of power rather than its sources, its intellectual methods and enunciative technique rather than its morality – to deconstruct rather than to destroy.[60]

It is possible to read the play The Last Carnival as an allegory of the historical/cultural development of Trinidad and Tobago, from Crown Colony to post-independence. This means that the characters represent certain attitudes, ideas, virtues and vices. Victor de la Fontaine represents French culture, Agatha Willett, British Law and Justice, Oswald the earthiness of Trinidad and the material base of that society, while George, Sydney and Jean represent African labour, human dignity and aspiration. Victor's children Clodia and Tony are citizens of the new nation and authentic inheritors of a syncretic culture. There is hardly a traditional plot as such. The conflicts inherent in these contending ideas vie for recognition and prominence in the allegorical mode. The use of allegory is a feature of post-colonial literatures. One writer contends that the allegory "emphasizes the importance of the language-place disjunction in the construction of post-colonial realities".[61]

The "language-place disjunction" is seen in the Imperial culture – its language, dance, food all are transported to a colony, not just of indigenous people, but transported people and the constricting dilemmas these create. The Last Carnival then is a rich metaphor for Walcott's plays since in them he deepens the exploration of the themes and counter-discursive strategies which are dear to him. He utilizes the techniques of the calypso, the music and rhythm of Caribbean language. The philosophical underpinnings of these themes are Walcott's view of history. He states: "In time the slaves surrendered to amnesia. That amnesia is the true history of the New World"[62] and the Adamic role of New World man which he postulates. The Adamic vision itself is a post-colonial strategy as it is committed to renaming what has already been named – thus altering the codes and subverting their central authority. Walcott reminds us that:

> *The great poets of the New World, from Whitman to Neruda, reject this sense of history. Their vision of man in the New World is Adamic. In their exuberance he is still capable of enormous wonder. Yet he has paid his accounts to Greece and Rome and walks in a world without monuments and ruins.*[63]

Walcott's view of history denies the role of victim to the descendants of slaves, and its attendant lust for revenge as it abhors the contrition of the master, these attitudes he believes produce bad art.

The opening scenes of The Last Carnival are paradigmatic of the post-colonial concern with the replacing of culture – the movement of Prospero outside society to the pastoral – the movement from the social to the natural. The New World in which cultural and linguistic practices are exposed to radical and subversive change. It is a sensuous world.

> *The light's astonishing. So clear! All this*
> *It's as if the world were making a fresh start.*[64]

It is an exotic, timeless world. It is a world where preconceptions must give way to a compelling new way of comprehending it. This is the world to which Victor de la Fontaine, French-Creole, effete artist, introduces British governess Agatha Willett. Victor needs someone to nurture his orphaned French-Creole children and chooses British Agatha Willett to do so. Thus will the French element of the society be colonized by the British as will the entire new society of Trinidad, and since Agatha Willett is colour blind, she will also make her imprint on the people of colour in her orbit. Sydney, symbol of the young black, restless facet of the society, will have the distinction of being her first target of the concept of egalitarianism. Walcott cleverly links his thematic concerns to these two major characters.

Victor de la Fontaine considers himself an impressionist, his obsession with Watteau, the French genre-painter (1684-1721) famous for his pictures of fetes-champetres and of shepherds and shepherdesses in the fashionable costume of the early 18th Century is contrasted with Agatha Willett's concern with the very real plight, of "those estate women, the ones in rags there working in the cocoa." This is the same Victor who warns Agatha that:

> *You'll look around you and all you'll see is fiction*
> *Some colourful backwater of the Empire.*[65]

Victor does not adjust his artistic vision to the realities of a tropical island, where women are dancing cocoa outside his window. He remains dinosaur-like, ready for extinction and irrelevance. What he admires in Watteau is his "stillness", his static decadence.

> *...He painted his whole culture as if it were a sunset; because all embarkation is a fantasy. You see those pilgrims in the painting? They can't move. It's like some paralyzed moment in a carnival.*[66]

But culture in a colonial situation, far from being a "sunset" or "static" is a battleground. It is a war in which political and ideological causes engage one another. So that when Victor portrays Monsieur Antoine Watteau at the masked carnival ball, he represents the "inheritors of France", and ironically is also representative of "You who take everything and contribute nothing/of which I am your elect." This scene foregrounds the allegorical opposition between the brothers, the Francophile/Trinidadian Victor/ Oswald. Oswald's coarse speech is deliberately transgressive, as it calls old Imperial norms into question.

> *So what the arse is I one must work to have this fete going? Jean, get your bam-bam off that step ladder, it have enough balloons, people thirsty. Vincent, wait! Mr Victor say he want them streamers to reach out quite to the pavilions on the lawn, so the light could catch them at sunset, and tell them damn steelband men no focking drinks till they play more tune. [Vincent exits] Jean! Come here! Now show me this new step girl. I say show me! You feel I too white to dance like all you black people or what? Eh, eh! Check this out [Dances] A-one, a-two, a-pang-alangalang. [Jean laughs but shows him the steps] Eh, eh, no more! You have a educated waist, girl. Le we fire one.*[67]

Oswald's use of language functions to construct "difference, separation and absence from the metropolitan norm." In discussing language in post-colonial literature there is general agreement that:

> ...*the English language becomes a tool with which a "world" can be textually constructed. The most interesting feature of its use in post-colonial literature may be the way in which it also constructs difference, separation and absence from the metropolitan norm. But the ground on which such construction is based is an abrogation of the essentialist assumptions of that norm and a dismantling of its imperialist centralism.*[68]

The battle that is being waged for cultural dominance is played out in the fiasco where Oswald is asked to read "what is this sad dark island? Cythera" and do a little skit of Toulouse Lautrec and Jane Avril (Agatha) amidst the bacchanal of a carnival masked ball. While Oswald does try t dissuade Victor from pursing this project, "give art a rest, this ain't theatre, this Carnival Mas! Oh, God." Needless to say the audience finds Oswald as Toulouse Lautrec his head buried under Agatha's skirt (Jane Avril's) much more to their taste. The Imperial Victor pours such scorn on them that it puts in perspective the opposition superior/inferior; Imperialist/native, albeit ironically.

> *You bitch! You vulgar little Cockney bitch!*
> *As for you, boy! Anything you see worthwhile,*
> *you think is your duty to coarsen and vulgarize,*
> *or jeer it to shreds, to creolize quality,*
> *and not recognize it. You don't have art —*
> *You hate me! You envy your own brother!*
> *It's not my fault that god gave me this gift.*
> *I don't envy your talent at arithmetic.*
> *But from the time she came here, simply because*
> *I was the one who chose her, because she's my property...*[69]

No, it is not envy which Oswald exhibits towards the Francophile, it is pride. He is proud of the sibling relationship between the Imperial culture and the syncretic carnival of Trinidad.

> *No, you arrogant bastard, you learn that!*
> *You learn from him what sacrifices mean*
> *You look, just look up from your work for a second,*
> *and see the pride he takes in you — not envy.*
> *The...pride...we both did what we did out there*
> *not to jeer at you, O Great Master, but*
> *to show them our contempt for mocking you.*[70]

Here is not rejection, no separation but an embrace of "difference and absence." One is quite proud to accept the brotherhood of culture. The theme of Independence is linked to the decline of the French cultural influence and the rise of the British, through the ritual of a cricket match. The ritual of hauling down the British flag is another element in the symbolic start of the new nation. Victor's previous observation resonates here, "all embarkation is a fantasy." The nation embarks on the adventure of nationhood. Is this mere illusion or reality? What exactly will change, what will be made new? The question of whether Independence is colonization in a new package will become a reality for the black power movement. Yet it is to Victor that we must return, a Victor whose wandering mind seems to flit between present and past, reality and illusion. He is not even sure who his brother is.

> ...Isn't this, ah, oh, so fête champetre, so Manet, so Manet! So...you are listening? Give her a boundary, Oswald! Hit him for six! [71]

It is Agatha who has to set him straight, "He's not batting, silly. He's at the other end." Victor in his madness is sure of one thing, that Oswald is "invented" in Trinidad. He is a Trinidad creation; while Victor is associated with images of death and sterility, foreshadowing his demise and his allegorical role as decadent French art. "But we can't change" (touching his groin) "So, nothing to run up the old flagpole, Willet!" "I am not an artist but a mortician." "And everything I touch with my brush is born dead." And "I felt you were striding towards me with a sword to cut off my head. To cut off my head," this is said to Agatha. Victor in his lucid moments recognizes that he has no role in the future young nation. Victor's suicide when it comes is not entirely surprising, he was already dead to the world around him, his power and dominance gone. He lives on in his children Clodia and Tony, whose creolization would not "vulgarize".

Clodia of In a Fine Castle and Clodia of The Last Carnival present a rich allegorical difference in role and function, and indicate the development of Walcott's historical and political perspective. While Brown of In a Fine Castle was simply flirting with the Creole Clodia, and swiftly abandoned the idea and remained uncommitted, it is Creole Clodia of The Last Carnival who confidently seduces Brown, very sure of his capitulation. She moves from a marginal role to a central, dominant role in the encounter. Walcott's flirtation with the "philosophy of creolization" is transformed into a willing seduction. Creolization is earthy, it is confident, this is well represented by the transgressive quality of Clodia's speech much like her uncle Oswald.

We're all going to bare our little boobs to the press. A piece of ass? I'm game. What am I supposed to do, seduce you?

But if I do anything, it is because I'm high, I'm independent and I feel like doing it. Do you want an imitation or a real de la Fontaine because you can have one now. Interested? [72]

Clodia the Creole is no imitation, she is genuine. She represents the transformative process, so does her brother Tony who, while dismissing his father as a "fraud", admits that "he made us cherish taste" albeit the wrong taste for the country. Yet he contributes his art in the culture of the new nation. Victor's contribution to the new nation cannot be underestimated, he is de la Fontaine, the fountain head, the source of the culture made vital, earthy, by the indigenous elements. Victor cannot "make them out" from the crowd. French culture is an integral part of the culture, appropriated by it, bearing the burden of the nation's experience.

Agatha Willett is the axis around which characters Jean Beauxchamps, Sydney and George, all African-Caribbean people revolve, in Walcott's exploration of the theme of a Caribbean identity. The British contribution to Caribbean identity is symbolized by her. She is characterized by her desire for justice, she is law and class solidarity. She assumes the "role of tutor to the new nation's children, not only the French Creoles." Jean Beauxchamps is her protégé while Sydney is encouraged and taught to be the equal of Clodia and Tony de la Fontaine. Agatha's reforming zeal is contrasted with Oswald's essentially conservative attitude to the changing status quo of black people. She is teaching Sydney, Jean and the old people about politics, the British Empire, village councils, principles of government. She insists on their rights and is distressed by the forced separation of the children after sunset. Oswald is quite clear where all this egalitarianism will lead.

You have Jean, a maid, calling me by my first name, or at least considering it. You had Sydney eating at the dining table with Clodia and Tony. You know who's going to suffer? Not you, not Clodia, not Tony, but Sydney. Anyway, George. . . [73]

Oswald's appeal to George here is instructive since George, who is portrayed as servile in In a Fine Castle and who arouses Brown's contempt is very much the same George of The Last Carnival. He is introduced to us as a man who not only knows his place but intends to have Sydney know this too. "Sydney, get your little black tail over here." This attitude is diametrically opposed to Agatha's and does precious little to aid the self-esteem of a young black child. So Agatha's "Damned if I'll be ruled by what George says!" is understandable.

Oswald despises Agatha's attempt at social engineering. She is a "do-gooder", a "communist", "Joan-of-Arc" "Missionary", "Miss Willett teaching little black pickney self-reliance." He declares that they need protection from her third class remorse. Maybe! But Agatha Willett is the genuine article, truly British law and justice in operation. She is conscious of her class affiliation to the workers, "know who lost the first war? The working class" she continues. "The ones who won were the officers and gentlemen." Agatha is of course planting the seeds of discontent in Sydney. "I'm going to teach them, Sydney's going to be more than a bloody groom!"

Jean Beauxchamps has been transformed from a maid to a Minister of Government in Independent Trinidad. One is struck by the fact that she is identified with loudness as though she is all "sound and fury" signifying nothing. Her coming is announced by the "Yoo-Hoo Aggie. Ozzie, you ready man, you coming?" One is struck by the change in relations between herself and Oswald who predicted this. "You have Jean, a maid calling me by my first name or at least considering it." He sees this as "democracy" – the levelling process. Jean's speech represents the "appropriation" of the Imperial language, the taking over of the language, remoulding it to new usages, separating it from the colonial privilege. Yet one is reminded that Agatha is the real power behind the Minister.

> *She moves Miss Beauxchamp anyway she likes.*
> *She'd make an excellent Prime Minister.*
> *Remote control of the colonies. Terrific.*[74]

Jean Beauxchamp is symbolic of the "Independent" nation's lack of independence, even their "Westminster" model of government is a hollow imitation which has not become an indigenous product, its economy is remotely controlled, and the expectations of the young, restless black citizens are doomed to disappointment.

Sydney is one of these disillusioned youths, tutored by Agatha Willett, and indoctrinated from childhood with the vision of equality with his white French-Creole master's children. He has flitted quite easily between manor and mean quarters, he has shown remarkable skill in handling horses; he is a groom and vicariously partakes in the sport of kings. We now see Sydney as a member of the Black Power Movement. For George, Sydney's uncle, it is "this Black power stupidness," for Clodia it is a masquerade, revolution is carnival.

> *Oh, God! Black Power, pang-alangalang! Che*
> *Guevara! Pang- alangalang!*

Go home, honkey, Pang- alangalang! You didn't hear!
Great, great! We passed right in front of here. Invaders
Steel band.[75]

For Oswald it is conundrum:

Black people don't know what the arse they want!
Country is a black country, the government black.[76]

From Brown:

...they use the words "ghettos" for what we called "lanes" or "alleys". The rhetoric
is as imported as their revenge; it lacks direction, despite the vehemence. I don't say you
aren't threatened, but what should have been an economic protest, a march of the shirtless
against urban injustice has turned into a Black power demonstration with berets, leather
jackets, another carnival.[77]

The identification of Black power with carnival is a clever device to
incorporate not only the metaphor of carnival as hybrid with its strange
and unpredictable mixture of attributes – as Creole, but to use the occasion
of carnival with its element of fantasy, with its "Back to Africa" band
to explore the quest of African Trinidadians for an authentic identity.
This phenomenon underscores the subversive element of carnival and by
extension the subversive quality of the text. It asserts the power of Black
writing and of post-colonial literature. It undermines the authority of the
establishment which denies and denigrates this ethnic reality. It implies the
author's distancing himself from a concept in which "a lot of people export
an idea of Africa out of both the wrong kind of pride and the wrong kind
of heroic idealism." [78] It treats as suspect the "importing" of rhetoric and
revenge, while questioning the sincerity of its advocates. The "tall black test
in a dashiki and afro" who spits at Clodia; the burning down of Santa Rosa,
are acts of revenge and of bitterness and are counter-productive. Yet the
Black power advocates in the hills are more concerned with the economics
of their situation and with sharing the wealth and product of their labour
and are not deceived by the "black country, black government" syndrome.

Eric Williams, former Prime Minister of Trinidad and Tobago notes:

It is one thing to get rid of colonialism on paper, but when it comes to removal of the
entrenchments of colonialism, that is where the real problem is.[79]

And Geddes Granger, the charismatic leader of NJAC and one of the
participants of the 1970 black Power upheavals in Trinidad states:

Too many of us are blinded by the constitutional disguises which give the appearance of Black people in control. This is the way the white power structure wants us to see it. The economic control which White people have gives them political control. Our politicians are turned into mere puppets. Once in every five years Black people get a little (very little in the set up) political bargaining status as election comes around. We are fed crash programmes and promises. Then the rest of the time is spent by the politicians bootlicking for the White power structure.[80]

While there is a touch of Romanticism in taking to the hills and changing a name to Africa Cuffy, the youths in the Black Power Movement are descendants of J. J. Thomas' Trinidadians from the "land of chronic agitation for Reform." C L R James observes of Caribbean people that they have been the most rebellious of people in history and that the colonization that was in existence in the West Indies well before the French Revolution of 1789 was very much dependent on them. He says:

I have found other evidence elsewhere and it seems to me that they, the slaves, ran that society; they were the persons responsible. If they had been removed the society would have collapsed. That is perfectly clear in certain writings about Trinidad and Tobago.[81]

In light of the sophistication of that society in the 18th Century, Sydney's inane observation in the 20th Century is almost anachronistic.

She should have leave that black boy alone, she shouldn't have shown him a place he couldn't reach. Or saddle some horse he wasn't supposed to ride, at least not as long as the race wasn't his." [82]

J. J. Thomas would be ashamed of him! There was no goal he would consider unreachable. Sydney needed to "disidentify" with any prescription of himself and to be truly liberated by embracing both the differences and absences and transforming them into limitless potential. National consciousness must be transported into social consciousness to be truly creative.

Agatha's remorse at Sydney's death is palpable. "We killed him. Didn't we George? Me, Mr Victor, Mr Oswald. Don't hang your head. Look at me; drive knives in my heart." She has not escaped change. Victor predicted it. Subtly but surely she does change.

She just couldn't resist the comforts of the estate once uncle Ozzie offered them to her. Maybe that's what she'd really wanted, not her equals but friendlier servants. Aggie was just like us! Avenging her background. I'd have done the same.[83]

Even Agatha's Britishness becomes creolized in the process; her paean of praise for the seductive Creole culture is a beautiful word picture of an age, its pure sensuousness a delight.

First she observed the customs of the house by being used to the customs of the house, its velvet habits, its mahogany surfaces where candles doubled themselves like mirrors during dinner. Her nails were tapered too, like candle flames, trembling with elegance and ebony servants in their silver service appeared like zombies to a small brass bell, circling a chair that she always set for Victor. The big four-poster, the white lace that lifted and settled down to silence with the roses. The sunlit satisfaction of that house. The mirrors drank her, all the outside world was vague as distance, shouts behind the clipped and muffled hedges of the house were like the faint sounds you hear from paintings, mice scratching at her mind. The house swallowed her like a cloud.[84]

The play ends where it began, at the Port-of-Spain docks. Arrivals and departure, immigration and emigration, our beginnings are in our endings and history is circular not linear. Life goes on. Clodia's departure is an act of affirmation, a desire to emulate the sense of mission of Agatha, her spiritual mother, for her spiritual son Sydney, Agatha prays that "Sydney's heart be the last ember left at Santa Rosa; let it not go out in all the other ashes." [85] Africa's descendants have earned their place in the land. The marginal, the "backwater" of Europe moves to the centre. Clodia the Creole takes over the mantle of the British Agatha her "sense of mission." A culture is transformed; historical perspectives foregrounded; and the movement from "backwater to centre stage do "jump-up" in The Last Carnival.

Experimental Broadway Musical Plays

DEREK Walcott's Trinidad Theatre Workshop, founded in 1966, was a vibrant dramatic force in the 70's. It had produced Ti Jean and other plays, it had taken Dream to New York and audiences were acclaiming the playwright's work. Walcott had begun to explore the possibility of putting his views on experimental musical plays into practice. He believed that song and dance could be thoroughly incorporated into the very design of the text. He was fortunate to have the enthusiastic services of Galt MacDermont who was willing to produce the musical scores. Walcott believed that O'Babylon! was the first real musical ever to be staged by his company. He felt that his performers should be judged by their singing and dancing as well as their ability to act. Both O'Babylon! (1978) and The Joker of Seville (1978) were used in these experiments although in the latter play singing and dancing were not as incorporated in the text. O'Babylon!, because of its Rastafarian theme and Jamaican setting, utilized reggae and spiritual lyrics, while The Joker of Seville, transplanted to Trinidad, employed the witty, risqué, calypso music. The Joker celebrates the sexual exploits of Don Juan and seems to fit more lightly into a musical mode, while some critics might find the beleagured Rastafarian predicament a bit heavy for a musical format, yet Walcott does manage to incorporate the music and the message well. Take this song for example.

> Where reggae come from?
> From fighting oppresser
> in Babylon, bruk them!
> From Emperor Selassie,
> Mock him and you Mock them!
> That's where reggae come from.

Say a man come from prison
And find him woman gone,
That's one of many reason
Why reggae was born
Why reggae was born
Why reggae was born.[1]

It underscores the conflict filled relationship of the marginal Rastafarian to his society as one of oppressor/oppressed. It names their deity Emperor Selassie, identifying their African connection, and it recognizes the creativity of the oppressed, the marginal, as a whole musical form is created.

O'Babylon! Relates the problems of a Rastafarian squatter group in Kingston, Jamaica and their quest for liberation from Babylon. They are inspired, by a visit from Haile Selassie of Ethiopia, to seek a return to Mother Africa. Because of their marginal status in the Community, they exist in a netherland of illegal activities and their passage to the Old World is stymied. Their faith holds them together despite the usual betrayals and the lure of materialism. They seek to subvert the hegemony of Imperial culture through their language, their religion and their isolationist tendency. This play embraces post-colonial themes such as the transformation of national consciousness to social consciousness in the quest for liberation. In this quest Haile Selassie dethrones the British Monarch and hierarchies are overturned so that communalism is privileged over capitalism, as is Africa over the New World and "I-an-I" over "We." They seek employment and dignity through their embrace of their African consciousness and history. Materialism is eschewed as they live simple lives while the realist/Anancy/Rude Bwoy figure embraces all – a very "creole" strategy – Rastafarianism, Garveyism, capitalism on his way to becoming the Big 'Black Star'. His success symbolizes the value of appropriation and hybridity, key post-colonial themes. Sufferer, the Christ figure, the spiritual man, contrasts with Rude Bwoy's materialism and represents the transcendence which man seeks. The establishment's desire to defuse and contain the energy of these natives is seen in their uprootment for the purpose of building the New Zion Hotel. Yet the play is ultimately concerned with courage, dignity and the power of love.

The Joker of Seville is a creolised version of Tirso de Molina's El burlador de Sevilla, set in a Spanish court. Walcott takes the opportunity to cross the Atlantic to set a Caribbean scene in Act I Scene 4. This scene with Tisbea the fisher-girl allows him the freedom to employ the witty, risqué double-entendre of the calypso genre.. Walcott expresses his enthusiasm for the challenge of adapting this play which celebrates Don Juan's escapades. This play is quintessential patriarchal discourse in which women are seen as property, as sexual objects which Don Juan can exploit. A feminist/womanist approach examines the Don Juan syndrome in terms of the sexual assumptions about women. One could then see the relevance of this examination in terms of male/female relationships in the Caribbean which might place less emphasis on women as sexual objects and more on the loving relationships between equal human beings.

Of course the success of these experimental Broadway musical plays will depend as much on the "musical" aspect as on the written texts and how well they are produced.

O'BABYLON!: A DISCOURSE ON MARGINALITY AS SOURCE OF CREATIVITY

The analogy which Houston A. Baker Jr. makes between the Structure of the black national text and the metaphor of maroonage as a state of constant warfare is applicable to O'Babylon!. This play looks at Jamaican Rastafarians whose lives must literally and figuratively epitomise this constant warfare between margin/centre, subculture/culture. Here Rastafarians attempt to "deconstruct" what they see as the power structures of English grammar and the hegemonic control by the British of black people. This "metaphor of maroonage" is stated thus:

> *The transgressive, invasive structure of the black 'national' text, which thrives on rhetorical strategies of hybridity, deformation, masking and inversion, is developed through an extended analogy with the guerrilla warfare that became a way of life for the maroon communities of runaway slaves and fugitives who lived dangerously and insubordinately on the frontiers or margins of all American profit and modes of production.*[2]

Thus both the text and the subject of O'Babylon! Are pursuing similar strategies; as post-colonial text O'Babylon! Resides on the periphery of the Imperial canon, both Rastafarians and text use their marginal status to dethrone the dominant British culture and make central the discourse on black emancipation. Rastafarians replace the British monarch by deifying the Ethiopian Haile Selassie and create a whole new culture in the process. This takes place in the context of resistance and opposition to the Babylonian, dominant culture of Jamaica. Language itself is transformed, becomes inclusive and empowering. By using "I" instead of "me" and "my" the Rastafarian stresses the fact that he is the subject of his own history.

The plural "we" is replaced by "I and I" which symbolizes both individual freedom and the unity of the Rastafarian community, based on the unity with Jah, God.

I-and-I shall be poor,
but, in I-and-I pride,
I-and-I rich with more
Revelation inside
Than who by the law
of Babylon abide,
O Babylon! [3]

The play's central theme is that of 'home' and 'belonging'. When the displacement of African peoples to the new world through slavery became problematic, the Imperialists sought ways to control and limit any form of creative, political involvement of the blacks in governing themselves. James Anthony Froude's main thesis is the "Contentment" of the blacks in the West Indies and his opposition to any form of political enfranchisement for them. The blacks were caught in-between, having no homeland and having not been given access to power in the new homeland.

J. J. Thomas in the preface of his book Froudacity, attacking Froude's thesis, states:

Overlarge and ever-increasing, so runs the argument – the African element in the population of the West Indies is, from its past history and its actual tendencies, a standing menace to the continuance of civilisation and religion. An immediate catastrophe, social, political and moral, would most assuredly be bought about by the granting of full elective rights to dependencies thus inhabited. Enlightened Statesmanship should at once perceive the immense benefit that would ultimately result from such refusal of the franchise. The cardinal recommendation of that refusal is that it would avert definitively the political domination of the Blacks which must inevitably be the outcome of any concession of the modicum of right so earnestly desired. [4]

In other words British Imperialism was not contemplating having a second Hayti in the region. Unlike the Black Jacobins the black British had no revolutionary slogan from the British metropole to motivate them to action, neither were they eavesdroppers of anything approaching the philosophical ferment of French Enlightenment – although they were aware of the debate about emancipation and the revolution of Hayti. They were thus left to agitate either for a return to Africa or control of these islands. It is thus not by accident that Marcus Garvey is a descendant of those Jamaican maroons, who were empowered by their guerrilla warfare with the British and who maintained strong African cultural customs. Home was Africa, this was essentially a reactive rather than proactive stance. It thrived in an atmosphere of separation, rather than syncreticity, of conflict – rather than reconciliation. It accentuated 'difference' without 'deference', and consigned itself to permanent marginality. It is through the language of the text that the marginal would become central not through the conflict. Said, notes these effects of "nativism."

Nativism, alas, reinforces the distinction even while revaluating the weaker or "subservient partner". And it has often led to compelling but demagogic assertions about a native past, narrative or actuality that stands free from the worldly time itself. One sees this in such enterprises as Senghor's negritude, or in the Rastafarian movement, or in the Garveyite back to Africa project for American Blacks, or in the rediscoveries of various unsullied, pre-colonial Muslim essences.[5]

Said's concern here is that "nativism" reinforces weakness and inferiority and becomes an otherworldly escape from the reality of present existence. In the case of Senghor's negritude Wole Soyinka's famous indictment of negritude is that glorification of the 'negro' is as contemptible as the injustice perpetuated against him, and furthermore Senghor uses the tools of French philosophical discourse to make his case of special pleading for the negro which subverts his intention. Walcott also attacks the assertion about a "native past", he observes:

> *The Caribbean very often refuses to cut the umbilical cord to confront its own stature. So that a lot of people exploit an idea of Africa out of both the wrong kind of pride and the wrong kind of heroic idealism. At great cost and a lot of criticism, what I used to point out was that there is a great danger in historical sentimentality. We are most prone to this because of the suffering of slavery. There's a sense of skipping the part about slavery and going straight back to a kind of Eden-like grandeur, hunting lions, that sort of thing. Whereas what I'm saying is to take the slavery, if you're capable of it without bitterness, because bitterness is going to lead to the fatality of thinking in terms of revenge.[6]*

In the case of the Rastafarians it is not so much revenge as it is alternatives, other peoples, other ways, other respect due. Yes, there is also "the wrong kind of heroic idealism". One still must confront the theme of "home" and "belonging" even as Brathwaite aptly puts it in the poem Postlude/Home.

Where then is the nigger's
home?
In Paris Brixton Kingston
Rome?
Here?
Or in Heaven?
What crime
his dark
dividing
skin is hiding?
What guilt
now drives him
on?
will exile never
end?
Will these spent
tears
Poor pauper's pence
earn him a little
solace here
bought if not given?
When the release
From fear, bent
back...[7]

Caught between the dilemma of the scattered diaspora, the necessity to avoid other wordly utopias, and the desire for belonging, what is one to do? If 'nativism' is a dead-end, then one must move beyond nativism by not confining oneself or limiting oneself to one's own sphere; one must, as Walcott suggests, take the facts of slavery "without bitterness", accept one's displacement, and embrace the limitless opportunities engendered by the Imperialist encounter with other cultures. True liberation is in transformation of social consciousness, and its concomitant modicum of dignity, from the black emancipationists' perspective, is part of the process of transformation. Cultural resistance laid the ground-work for self-determination and national independence. It is this role that the Rastafarian movement and its hermeneutics played, and it continues to play an important role in the process of transforming national consciousness. Out of the embrace of Africa and Garveyism has sprung Bob Marley and his message in song of emancipation from "mental slavery'; the old Imperialist script of self depreciation and negation and the inferior status of the black man led to considerable research of the Bible and ancient African history which helped to empower generations to accept themselves and their full potential as human beings. This was no frivolous embrace of a "lion hunting" romantic notion of Africa, this was a call to refuse and refute the Imperialist script on Africa, to re-examine the African script about Mali and Timbuktu and the kingdoms of Ghana. It recognises that African history did not begin with slavery in the New World. After this comes either the greater liberation or the limitation which comes from a refusal to take the leap from national consciousness to social consciousness.

An understanding of Rastafarian theology is crucial to the deconstruction of its discourse. When, in November 1930, Rastafari Makonnen was crowned Emperor of Ethiopia and took the name Haile Selassie and received the titles "King of Kings", "Lord of Lords" and conquering Lion of the Tribe of Judah", some people thought that Garvey's prophecy had been fulfilled. Poor uneducated people in the difficult crisis of the 30's saw the new Emperor of Ethiopia as their redeemer. In the slums of Kingston, the Authorized version of the Bible was consulted and proof texts were found for the Divinity of the Haile Selassie in Rev. 2:2-5 "Weep not, behold, the lion of the Tribe of Judah, the root of David hath prevailed to open the book and to loose the seven seals therefore". Psalm 68:31 also spoke clearly to believers. "Princess shall come out of Egypt, and Ethiopia shall stretch forth her hands unto God", as did passages like Ezel.37:17 and Rev. 19:16.

In Rastafarian theology Selassie is God, and Babylon, the land of captivity stands for the whole complex of attitudes which humiliate the black man and hold him captive.

This interpretation of the Bible is a post-colonial, counter-discursive one. Rastafarianism is thus deconstructing canonical codes. The divinity of Haile Selassie runs counter to imperial interpretation of the Bible. It is thus a strategy to overcome the power of the Imperialist values. The capital of Babylon thus becomes Rome. Ethiopia is Zion, the place of salvation, the Promised Land – heaven is here and now. The commandments include, as Sufferer says in the first scene of O'Babylon!:

> ...*You shall not eat salt.*
> *the flesh of the sow, and the sow's litter*
> *Shall to you be obscene; the woman, your sister*

Shall always obey you. You shall believe
that the Emperor Selassie, Jah Rastafari,
Lion of Judah and King of King, is the one God.[8]

Essentially then this picaresque play pits against each other two seemingly opposing perceptions, which seek to find answers to the dehumanising legacy of imperialism: should the Blackman seek emancipation through a pursuit of materialism, or should he seek the imperatives of a dignified authentic existence? This is really a contrived debate, since everyone knows that they are not mutually exclusive goals. The cynic might add that one does not have to prove one's humanity to anyone. Ostensibly the characters Rude Bwoy and Aaron represent the apparent dichotomy – Rude Bwoy is the "Big Black Star", the name resonates with Garvey's major economic venture – The Black Star Line.[9] Clearly Rude Bwoy is identified with that aspect of Garvey's philosophy. He embodies the idea of economic self-sufficiency, the pursuit of material well-being. He also functions as the voice of reality and acts as a counterfoil to esoteric Rastafarianism. Aaron represents the search for black dignity, which the Rastafarian philosophy supplies, but that does not mean that Rastafarianism is not also seeking material self-sufficiency, so while these two characters seem to represent opposing attitudes, there are certain overlaps which suggest a continuum, not oppositions/hierarchial positions. This conflict is played out against the background of the New Zion Construction Company's prior claim to the land on which the community squats. One ought to pause a while to deconstruct the New Zion's construction Company's prior claim. Whose priority are we speaking of? Imperialism's/Captialism's or Native's/Community's claims? The tunnel vision of the Imperialist's/New Zion Construction Company permits one to see the same sinister colonial motive – to absorb, contain, defuse, detoxify, the creative energy of the brethren so that they remain marginal. One remembers Froude's claim that the natives were "sleek, contended". He could not see them as political agitators, for fear that they would dominate, become empowered to determine their fate. He constructs a persona for them which negates other possibilities, other potentials. It is this "construction" which Rastafarians seek to dismantle, dethrone.

It is quite clear from the start of the play that the metaphor of "broken people" attests to their marginal status; they are the wretched of the earth.[10]

I collect broken people like I collect bottles.
And you was a bottle filled with the wrong spirit.[11]

Sufferer's identification with a Messianic role is evident, but it is also clear why they are broken people. Rude Bwoy is peddling ganja and Rufus is a violent man.

> *Now Rufus had this razor*
> *That him christened "Mabrak".*
> *Him could make it blaze, Sir,*
> *like lighting slice the dark.*
> *But who live by the razor*
> *shall perish by the gun,*
> *and Rufe, him was a dealer*
> *in the streets of Babylon.*[12]

Yet they will take divergent paths and Rude Bwoy's path leads unwaveringly from ganja pusher to realizing his dream of becoming a "Big Black Star". This transformation is achieved through characterization. Rude Bwoy is seen as the trickster voice of reality driven single-mindedly by his ambition. Albeit fascinated by the philosophy of the Rastafarians, he fears that a commitment to its discipline and world view is antithetical to his ambitions. He recognises its limitations. This does not prevent him from making use of their ideas, however, which are relevant to his talents and ambitions. Rude Bwoy symbolises the concept of hybridity, creolisation, his masking and "maroonage" mentality, his dangerous and insubordinate life, lived "on the frontiers or margins of all American profit and modes of production,"[13] ensure for him the centre stage, move him away from the very marginality which supports his creative energies.

> *'Ail Queen O Sheba, Ethiopia's pride,*
> *Lift you 'ead 'igh, You ain't bound to hide,*
> *Come mek me take you fro a chariot ride.*[14]

Rude Bwoy's creativity taps into the Rastafarians' pride in Ethiopia to "hustle the weed" among the brethren, in pursuit of his materialistic goals, he rejects their concern with the spiritual life.

> *...Me don't have a soul.*
> *When we make a big pile back in Babylon,*
> *me promise to help you.*[15]

He is sceptical of Rastafarian theology.

> *How this lickle black man could be God.*[16]

in reference to Haile Selassie. Not surprisingly when he achieves his ambition it leaves a hollow feeling.

> I get a hollow feeling, now I've won.
> I never thought that I
> would envy Aaron,
> one man to stand alone
> against all Babylon,
> lose everything him own
> and still stay strong as stone;
> that calls for more admiration
> than my own.
> But I'm a big black star,
> a big, black star.[17]

Is this a rude awakening for Rude Bwoy? There are things which money cannot buy, like strength of character, and that sense of fulfilment that is the reward for conquering great odds, odds such as Aaron's penchant for impulsive violent responses. Aaron's road to self-awareness and to his unshakeable faith is a devious one.

> 'Me never see God neither. But Him exist.[18]

His conversion to Rastafarian does not immediately result in a better temper or a better relationship with Priscilla whom he loves. "I love you, then, the same Adam love Eve".[19] Priscilla, the former Miss Electric Gyal, a night club singer can attest to this:

> Lord, me wish you was Rufus for true! 'Cause
> God knows you treat me gentler as a Criminal
> than now, when you "good"! You don't love God.
> You is vex with Him, so you raging with me.[20]

He is a self-confessed "man of anger" who abandoned possession: Dolly regrets his new status thus:

> But ahead was a promising criminal career.[21]

Aaron's chisel is a metaphor of his life, as he applies what was his burglar's tool to the sculptor's craft; Aaron's redeeming feature is his incredible resilience, his ability to seek forgiveness and to start all over again.

One can see both the transformation of Rude Bwoy to Black Star and Aaron to Sculptor as paradigmatic of the creative process, which not only empowers Rastafarianism but which informs the strategy of the post-colonial writer. It is the creative adaptation/adaptability which defies easy conscription into the Imperialist definitions and designs. There are interesting parallels between O'Babylon! and Dream on Monkey Mountain, where the Rastafarian/Babylon/Capitalist conflict is replaced by the folk/colonialist conflict, there is the Back to Africa discussion in both, and of course, there are the transformations of Rude Bwoy/Aaron in O'Babylon! and Lestrade in Dream. Finally there is betrayal, Moustique's betrayal of the dream for material gain is echoed in Rude Bwoy's betrayal of the dream for Stardom. In the hiatus following the negotiations of the New Zion Construction Company to remove the squatters, all the forces of Babylon are ranged against them. Dewes, Mrs Powers, "aptly named" Deacon Doxy. Dewes' ironic "these people are armed/with a dangerous doctrine; love" and "Bunch of bloody idlers", set the stage for Mrs Powers tutelage by Rude Bwoy, a tutelage which feeds her prejudices. "These are somewhat violent types here, but…I am in your power, Mrs Powers." Deacon Doxy is as much a political caricature as any one can be:

> *Ginnal, ginnal, and samfie man,*
> *What is his name?*
> *Chorus: Politican!* [22]

It is as cruel a bit of irony as one could imagine for those forces of faceless Imperialism/Capitalism, which are behind the venture to displace this community of poor people, to be called "New Zion", when one considers that Zion is the name of the Rastafarians' heaven. Heaven/Capitalism, Hell/Rastafarianism are precisely the binary oppositions which Deacon Doxy projects.

> *Don't tell me about some drug-induced heaven*
> *The heaven I'm building*
> *is there a meal a day,*
> *a roof over our heads.*[23]

Except, of course, that Deacon Doxy's credibility as a disinterested philanthropist is quite low, and his targets do not take this 'Greek bearing gifts' seriously. His real function is to bribe Sufferer and company to leave and thus to condemn them to terminal marginality with a promise that they will be part of the quota of persons to visit Ethiopia when Selassie visits.

People over sixty and those with criminal records would not be eligible. This effectively eliminates Sufferer. Doxy is however willing to move heaven and earth to get the over sixty Sufferer on the trip. Aaron is unmoved by his offer:

> ...but if them brand me criminal,
> Then me shall remain criminal.[24]

Aaron, true to his word, stumbles once more on his private road to Damascus, he almost forfeits Priscilla's love and trust by succumbing to his daemon and burning down the New Zion Construction Company. He is defended by Goldstein who in bemoaning the injustices of poverty sees Aaron:

> Starlike, a diamond, unquenchable,
> A simple spark! [25]

Despite prison and the disappointment of not seeing Haile Selassie, one suspects that with Priscilla's loyalty and love, his "Zion a Come". His wholeness and integrity have been tested and proven. His strength is in overcoming. His retreat to the hills has been seen as a "nebulous vision" by Hamner:

> Walcott would have done well to have developed those forces in Aaron's life that give
> him the strength to believe, rather than trail off into a nebulous vision of future rewards
> in Zion.[26]

Walcott is well aware of the "heroic idealism" of men like Aaron, but why deny the need of the 'transcendent ones to retreat to their mountain experiences', after all maroons also inhabited mountain terrain without retreating from the struggle for empowerment. As a musical the play works, since the reggae rhythms, the lyrics and the choruses are integral elements of plot development and characterisation, for example Deacon Doxy's song.

> Yes, it's the Jonah-in-the-whale situation,
> its happening to every little nation.
> Co-operate with them big corporation
> or else: more poverty, more degradation!
> That's it, friends,
> That's what it means.[27]

This reference is to Jonah, a prophet of God, who is asked to go to Nineveh, that great city and "cry against it, for their wickedness is come before me". Jonah tries to run away from his mission, by taking the ship to Tarshish. This act of disobedience creates such a tempest that the ship's master asks the sleeping Jonah to arise and call upon his God that they do not perish. As they plead with him to tell them what they should do, he says, "Take me up, and cast me forth into the sea;" it is said that the Lord had prepared a great fish to swallow up Jonah. He spent three days in the belly of the whale. It is "out of the belly of hell" that he cries to the Lord God, who releases him from the whale unto dry land. Jonah repents of his disobedience and returns to Nineveh but the King and people of Nineveh repent of their wickedness, and God does not destroy them. Jonah is angry with God for his forgiveness of Nineveh.

Two lessons are learnt by Jonah, he learns that a prophet should be obedient and that God's purposes of grace are not necessarily limited to the chosen people. God is compassionate. Ironically 'Prophet' Doxy is obedient to the God of the "big corporation", to the status quo. He does their work willingly unlike Jonah's disobedience to God's will. Deacon Doxy works for the same forces which Jonah was asked to cry against in Nineveh that great city; the powerful establishment. Doxy on the other hand sees "more poverty, more degradation" if one does not obey the Corporate "God". Men are not simply pigs to be fed. Jonah, like Doxy, must learn of God's unlimited grace to all people, not simply chosen people, but especially people like the Rastafarians and repentant Ninevehans. This guilt/victim status which Deacon Doxy identifies with and cooperates with may warrant his release from "the whale" of protective self-deception, which blinds him to his true function as Imperialist/Capitalist lackey. Deacon Doxy thus stands in contra-diction to the strategy of the play since, his uncreative sterile acceptance of Imperialism's hegemony is directly opposed tot eh creativity of Rude Bwoy and Sufferer. The playwright, like Rude Bwoy and Sufferer, employs the strategies of hybridity, appropriation and "creolisation" to subvert this hegemony. They move out of the shadowy margins and catapult themselves to centre stage by doing so. The liberation which they seek comes from the creative centre, as Rude Bwoy's song suggests:

> *Where reggae come from?*
> *from fighting oppressor*
> *in Babylon, bunk them!*
> *From Emperor Selassie,*
> *mock him and you mock them!*
> *That's where reggae come from.*

Say a man come from prison
and find him woman gone,
that's one of many reasons
Why reggae was born.
Why reggae was born —
Why reggae was born.[28]

Rude Bwoy's song reinforces the concept of culture as conflict, as the history of Jamaica shows. It is the "maroon" metaphor at work. It is critically and creatively structuring one's reality while fighting the oppressor. Rude Bwoy is a symbol of true liberation of limitless opportunities grasped, as he incorporates calypso, Reggae and Jazz in his songs. He embraces the transformation which comes from going beyond national consciousness. The text O'Babylon! must be seen as the objective correlative of a "Rude Bwoy", it would not be confined to the margins, the periphery of the Imperial canons.

The situation at the end of the play, then, bears out Edward Said's contention that liberation, as an intellectual mission, has shifted from the comfortable centre to the margins:

Yet it is no exaggeration to say that liberation as an intellectual mission, both in the resistance and opposition to the confinements and ravages of imperialism, has now shifted from the settled established and domesticated dynamics of culture to its unhoused, decentred and exilic energies, whose incarnation today is the migrant and whose consciousness is that of the intellectual and artist in exile, the political figure between domains, between forms, between homes and between languages. From this perspective then all things are indeed counter, original, spare, strange.[29]

THE JOKER OF SEVILLE: A FEMINIST/WOMANIST PERSPECTIVE

Feminism has a wide spectrum of meanings and manifestations, as political, cultural and theoretical constructs. These are feminists, African feminists, Lesbian feminists, Asian and Arab feminists, and European feminists. Politically there is the controversial notion of equality which seeks opportunities in terms of education, merit and rewards, and the social consequences of such equality. Political constructs tend to differentiate between the experiences of women in developed versus undeveloped societies. The role of race and class is crucial in confronting the hegemony of white, Euro-American middle-class feminism. The voice of black, working class, Third-world women is recognised as crucial to the ongoing feminist dialogue, as is the African-American feminist voice. The African feminist Chukwenge Oqunyemi advocated the separation of black and white feminism by coining the term "womanism", a feminism for her which must be interpreted strictly on racial lines. Thus feminism as perceived by African women is linked to anti-colonial, anti-racist struggles in places like Namibia and South Africa. African feminists seek the right to life as free women and complete social beings. Feminism is not defined by them in terms of man-hating. A similar phenomenon is observed in African-American and Caribbean feminists' positions, it is inclusive rather than exclusive, it also seeks the support and liberation of the male. This inclusiveness is what separates the feminists "from the womanist" position.

Alice Walker, the African-American writer used the new term "womanist". It is a commitment to the survival and wholeness of an entire people, female and male as well as to a valorization of women's works in all their varieties. She is committed to turning the idea of art on its head. In an essay "In search of our Mothers' Gardens", she asked the question, "What is my literary tradition?" She included in her tradition the women who transformed the material to which they had access into their conception of beauty; the cooks, the gardeners, the quilters, the storytellers. She reclaimed the foremothers. She pointed to a critical approach, for she believed that art, and the thought and sense of beauty on which it is based, is not only the province of those with a room of their own, or those in libraries, universities and literary Renaissances, but it is also the province of those who work in kitchens and factories those who nurture children and adorn homes, harvest crops, type in offices and manage them. Womanist inquiry also assumes it can talk both effectively and productively about men, since African-American women writers have had to carry on a dialogue with the phallocentric writing by black males which perpetuates stereotypes of black women.[30] In this regard, note Walcott's portrayal of the black woman Mabel, in Remembrance, in contrast to the Englishwoman, Miss Hope. Caribbean women critics, in seeking a definition of their own role and theoretical moorings in the selection of essays in Out of the Kumbla, edited by Carole Boyce Davies and Elaine Savory Fido, have similar concerns; we note, for example, Sylvia Wynter's questioning of the absence of Caliban's mate as an alternative sexual-erotic model of desire in Caribbean literature – or in any literature for that matter.[31]

Within the African-American feminist camp there is the added concern that the burden the black woman bears is celebrated in terms such as "she is already liberated", which, to some, romanticizes "marginality" and is seen as an excuse for placing her needs last. Is she free to be forever burdened by low income, low status, and single child rearing? This "liberation" seems designed to cover up female disenfranchisement, exploitation, oppression and despair. As one perceptive feminist noted, the difference between the sexes is not whether or not one does not have a penis, it is whether or not one is an integral part of a phallic masculine economy. This brings us to Freud whose towering influence on Feminist theoretical discourse stems from his famous dictum on women. Women, he asserted, were passive, narcissistic, masochistic and penis-envying; they were less morally conscientious than men.[32] Freud's theory thus elevated to a central position in the discourse, the phallus, as symbol of male power and authority; thus God, father, state, order, property and law are signifiers of the phallus, together with which they constitute the corner-stone of patriarchal discourse. Women, on the other hand are relegated to remaining powerless, penis-envying, castrating beings, aware of their loss and thus cowed into silence.

While feminist criticism has flourished in combining every critical approach, I would like to examine the relevance of two feminist theorists, Julia Kristeva and Luce Irigaray; they both counter the phallus/symbolic theory with a material/semiotic theory; thus positing the binary oppositions of phallus/material, symbolic/semiotic. Basically their theory launches an assault on the hegemony of patriarchal ideas and the dominant discourse in male literary experiences; this theory seeks to reconstruct a female perspective and experience in an effort to change the tradition that has silenced the woman, or made her unknown to herself. The patriarchal construct privileges physical/sexual aggression, heroic conquest and intellectual domination.

Kristeva in her book La Revolution du Langage Poetique proposes the term "semiotic" which is the opposite of symbolic. She means by this a pattern or play of forces which one can detect inside language and which represents a sort of residue of the pre-oedipal phase, the pre-verbal moment, when the child is bound up with, and dependent on, the mother's body. The phase when instinctual drives are organized and rhythmic models developed. Irigaray elaborates on the idea f the maternal metaphor, the difference it explores, in relation to the patriarchal construct. It suggests a strategy of "getting within, seizing powerfully, manipulating male discourse on women".[33] Irigaray in her book, An Ethics of Sexual Difference, states:

If traditionally and as a mother woman represents place for man, such a limit means that she becomes a thing, with some possibility of change from one historical period to another. She finds herself delineated as a thing. Moreover the maternal feminine also serves as an envelope, a container, the starting-point from which man limits his things.[34]

She maintains that woman should distinguish herself from both the envelope and the thing, that is from her function as envelope/womb and as form as thing/person, creating some interval or play, something in motion and unlimited, which disturbs man's perspective, his world and his limits. But, she observes, because he fails to leave her a subjective life, and to be on occasion her place and her thing, in an intersubjective dynamic, man remains within a master-slave dynamic. The slave, ultimately of a God on whom he bestows the characteristics of an absolute master.

Secretly or obscurely, he is a slave to the power of the maternal-feminine which he diminishes or destroys. Irigaray takes Freud's dictum that woman is identified with orality, to observe that morphologically she has "two mouths and two pairs of lips", and that she can act on this morphology or make something of it only if she preserves her relation to spatiality and to the fetal. Although she needs these dimensions to create a space for herself (as well as to maintain a place for the other) they are traditionally taken from her to constitute man's nostalgia and everything that he constructs in memory of this first and ultimate dwelling place.

She notes man's endless construction of a number of substitutes for his prenatal home, from submarines to skyscrapers. In exchange he sometimes buys her a house, even shuts her up in it, places limits on her that are the opposite of the unlimited site in which he unwillingly situates her. She speaks of containment and envelopment of woman within walls while man envelopes himself and his things within her flesh. The nature of these envelopes is not the same: on the one hand, invisibly alive, but with barely perceivable limits; on the other visibly limiting or sheltering but at the risk of being prison-like or murderous if the threshold is not left open. Irigaray concludes that man must reconsider the whole question of our construct of place, but, in order to move to another age of difference, and in order to construct an ethics of the passion, suggests that we need to change the relations between form, matter, interval and limit, an issue that has never been considered in a way that allows for a relationship between two loving subjects of different sexes.

The maternal metaphor opposes the symbolic language – the language of the patriarchal discourse as sure, self-identical truth – with the semiotic which is fluid and plural, a kind of pleasurable creative excess, over precise meaning and it takes "sadistic" delight in destroying or negating such signs.

Thus while the dominant discourse is symbolized by man who orders, punishes, asserts, demands, commands, reasons, describes, narrates, states, collects, organizes, the semiotic is reflected in Irigaray's statement —

> ...woman for her part, chats, tattles, gossips, weaves invention, fables, myths. She exchanges the meaning of exchange without having any object.[35]

One of course must challenge the notion of "creative excess over precise meaning", for the discourse which must take place by feminists in terms of the dominant discourse must be couched in precise language or run the risk of further trivialising their contribution to intellectual discourse. One must refute the arrogance of the dominant discourse not by imprecision but in clear terms, yet in a creative way. Women must challenge Freud's dictum that they are masochistic, not only because Freud's views were neither as rational nor as disinterested as his work may seem, but because we must recognise that Freud's unconscious desires also precluded the objectivity he might have been reaching for. Freud's masochistic label tends to produce a rationale for those myths which identify woman with the perversity of deriving pleasure from pain or, humiliation, it is the foundation of the notion that women love to be beaten as proof of love or that they contribute to their rape. One will consider how this notion functions in the patriarchal discourse of The Joker of Seville. One does delight in destroying or negating such signs.

A feminist/womanist perspective for me is self-evident. Both feminists and womanists seek to unsilence women, to give voice to women's perception of the world they inhabit. Both recognise the power of discourse and the way the dominant discourse with its language of authority, control and certainty tends to neutralise a more tentative female approach to discourse, precisely because the dominant discourse pretends to see little value in what women have to say, or, indeed seeks to trivialise what they do say. The womanist concern with the stereotyping of black women in literature by black male writers and the need to talk effectively and productively with such writers in order to uplift all black people, is only different in emphasis form the Euro-American feminists' concern with women's portrayal in literature generally. The womanists' embrace of all women's attempt to make a thing of beauty of an in their lives, and not simply to privilege those who walk within the halls of academia recognizes all the efforts of silenced women and have worked towards unearthing all those oft times hidden jottings, poems, quilts, and embroideries. Feminism in all its varieties seeks to construct a theoretical framework while being mindful of the ways in which the dominant discourse about class, race, underdevelopment, economics may impinge on that venture. All feminism is about the empowerment of women.

The Joker of Seville is couched in the language of the cocksure, by which those who wield sexual and social power maintain their grip. Fathers dispose of daughters in the best traditions of the age of chivalry. The women are "enveloped" and "contained" shut up within courts, castles or convents and locked in the master-slave situation by men who are secretly afraid of the power of the maternal-feminine, which they try to diminish or destroy. God, law, the father and property all are invoked to keep her in servitude. Don Juan appears in the ironic role of "liberator" of women and one who "honours" them.

> *My faith? the faith of all women.*
> *Woman's religion is love.*
> *They will resurrect me again.*
> *Imprisoned by laws, everyone*
> *Idealises a liberator*
> *lying next to lover or husband,*
> *and their dream is my creator.*[36]

Clearly Don Juan's mission has nothing to do with either liberation or honour, rapists can see their role as liberators of women. It has more to do with conforming to, and reinforcing a view of woman that relegates her to the Freudian perversity of the masochist, of passive sufferer, of defenseless/ wounded, as castrating/powerless.

Walcott participates in this dominant discourse in his adaptation of Tirsa de Molina's El Burlador de Sevilla, with unseemly gusto, and confirms the view of him as "Soul Brother to the Joker of Seville"; mind you, this is not my terminology. This is the Trinidad Guardian of November 6, 1974, the headline for an article written by the author himself on the play's production in Port-of-Spain, Trinidad. While it is not my terminology, my assessment of the adaptation confirms the Brotherhood of the genre with Sparrow's "Village Ram" (1964) in which he valorises the rampaging male, and more recently "The more the Merrier" (1992). Walcott, interestingly, says:

> *Yet without knowing Tirso's speech, I felt a contemporary, provincial, and immediate enthusiasm, for his play, because of Trinidad. The wit, panache, the swift or boisterous élan of his period, and of the people in his play, are as alive to me as the flair and flourishes of Trinidadian music and its public character.*[37]

Other works which developed the theme are Shadwell's The Libertine, a play, Byron's poem 'Don Juan' and G. B. Shaw's 'Man and Superman.' Mozart's musical skills are also brought to bear on the theme.

The lyrical quality of much of the play makes it an enjoyable evening's entertainment at the theatre, that is if one also enjoys the modus operandi of the Don Juans of the world. Through disguise and trickery he seduces four women. His first seduction is of Isabelle. He is disguised as her lover Octavio; his second seduction, that of Tisbea, Walcott places in a fishing village across the Atlantic in the Caribbean; his third seduction is of Ana, Don Gonzalo's daughter. This he carries out in her father's house, disguised as her chosen lover, the Marquis de Mota. This results in a duel where Don Gonzalo dies in defending his daughter's honour. This final conquest, the most distasteful, takes place on Aminta's wedding day, she is tricked into believing that her brand-new husband has given her up in Don Juan's favour. In the end Don Juan is killed as Ana avenges her father's death.

Don Juan's obsessive behaviour in honouring women with dishonour, constitutes man's obedience to subconscious impulses. Both the desire to defy prohibitions such as those imposed in Eden, and the desire to return to the womb. This obsession needs to be replaced by a conscious decision to change the nature of the relationship between men and women from one of power and violence to one of mutual love and respect. But make no mistake about it, this play, which takes place near a cemetery, and the action of which (according to the author's direction) would have the audience seated "as in a rural bullfight, cockfight, or stickfight", is no joke — it is unmistakably a play about sex as violence and the perpetuation of violence against women by macho men who refuse to acknowledge woman's complexity; thus Don Juan represents everyman who vicariously partakes of the myth of the female rape-complex; that is that a woman wishes to be raped. This viewpoint refuses to see rape as violence: Nothing attests more to the powerlessness of women, than their denial of choice in who penetrates them. If a woman has no control over what happens to her body she is totally impotent.

> *I just stood*
> *There, soiled and speechless with its seed.*[38]

Says Ana, one of Don Juan's victims. This play glorifies "phallocentric privilege",[39] and is a slap in the face of women, since woman is more than anatomical sex. One must pause to consider how much the humor in the play revolves around sexual fantasies. One would expect an audience of men and women to react differently to sexually explicit jokes. By and large men might enter into the fantasy of sexual violence and find it titillating, exciting and funny. Generally women might find it embarrassing and while some men might see it as humorous, most women might find it an affront to women, as it portrays them as vulnerable and powerless, objectifying them rather than making them subjects who determine their fate. One must be cautious in stating that most women would react consciously, that is in terms of the gender stereotyping. In a Caribbean context it has been acknowledged that many women enjoy and applaud when male calypsonians sing not only calypsos that are disparaging of women, but also those that treat the subject of violence aginst women as justifiable. Gender relationships are still relationships of power, naked power, and are inextricably tied up with women's economic power, or lack thereof. The "woman as property" mindset still exists, despite women's social, educational and economic strides. Is Caribbean society a macho society, less sensitive to rape or to violence against women? If it is so, it is cause for concern. Consider Don Juan, then, as everyman's alter ego. Octavio's disturbing dream supports this view.

> *There is a garden. In its bush*
> *a woman sprawls to greet the snake,*
> *its adzehead muzzling her bush.*
> *My cold sweat turns to scales just like*
> *the thing I would abhor. I change*
> *into the serpent, too, sometimes,*
> *and it's my body and not Juan's*
> *that wraps her. God, she groans, she seems*
> *to worship her seducer!*
> *Mixed in the muck of that dream*
> *I cannot call my motives pure.*[40]

This archchetypal dream is littered with images of the fall of man. "The garden", the "snake", the "serpent": Adam's fall from grace is attributed to Eve. She "sprawls to greet the snake". The burden of Adam's fall rests on Eve's shoulders, she seems/to worship her seducer: In other words she is responsible for her rape. This theory of original sin has always conveniently given man the right to be irresponsible. Eve is a convenient scapegoat.

The master plot of the invention [of Eve and Adam] exists on the condition that Eve "read" the world only one way, by making herself the mirror of patriarchal authority.[41]

Eve, the embodiment of forbidden sexuality, is forever imprisoned by a patriarchal Judeo-Christian theology in the role of a possession. She must accept punishment and the control of male authority, since her power to tempt man is a dangerous force. She must now "read" the world in one way. She must reflect this by submitting to this authority and power. The essential conflict of the play is the tension which exists between two perceptions of woman; first there is woman as "anatomical sex" that is as sexual object. She is "no more than an indifferent/slit to take another stiff";[42] and secondly, woman as possession, reflection of "patriarchal authority". She is the conduit of heirs to male wealth and privilege. The whole force of tradition, religion, chivalry is behind this perception. Thus marriage is the acceptable mode for the perpetuation and glorification of woman's subject state. So that Gonzalo can say:

> Seville is rich only if she,
> Like my own daughter, still obeys
> God, king and Father.[43]
> And the King of Castile can arrange a marriage for Gonzalo's daughter.
> ...I give your daughter's hand:
> A young and supple-tempered blade,
> Juan Tenorio, Diego's son.[44]

These two perceptions of women are only threatened by the woman who aggressively accepts and enjoys her sexuality. In this unashamedly macho context death seems to be the only fate for such a being. Tisbea's fate is drowning. She seems not only to be an intellectual, but one who accepts her sexuality. On seeing Juan and Catalimon on the beach she recognises her awakening sexuality:

> Oh, the tempest that's seething
> in me, I shall burst!
> See the heave of this bosom.
> O dark heat in this bust,
> O wonderful morning,
> can this be lust?[45]

The real irony of The Joker of Seville is that the joke is finally on Juan himself, since his inability to love and his betrayal of women, by refusing to accept them on terms other than "indifferent slits", make his encounters with them sterile and, while placing them in the role of victims, allows them creative responses such as compassion, forgiveness and resolve:

> I thought it was desire, not knowing

till now that it was something else,
The love which surrenders loving
to become love. Its name is grace.
And I had owed this power to Juan.[46]

This is Isabella's response to her violation by Don Juan. Don Juan also disturbs the moral order and this leads to chaos, since the irresponsibility of his behaviour and the need to deceive allow him to operate in an immature, pre-rational and instinctive manner. This anarchic behaviour is the stuff of which dreams are made, it does not lend itself to productive authentic existence. Robert Hamner observes:

Juan embodies an irrational force — the spirit within man which urges him to obey subconscious impulses and to defy prohibitions such as those imposed in Eden and in society. He is, as existential, post Adamic man, outside the pale of institutional values. The terms of his quest, indeed of his very existence, require that he use every trick in his arsenal to outmaneuver each man and conquer each female he encounters.[47]

Juan himself recognises this instinctual force:

I serve one principle! That of
The generating earth whose laws
Compel the loping lion to move
Toward the fallow lioness,
Who in this second embodied
His buckling stagger! I
Fought for that freedom delivered
After Eden. If I defy
Your principles because I served
Nature, that was chivalry
Less unnatural than your own.[48]

Don Juan recognises in his self-justification for his own behaviour, the conflict between his behaviour and the establishment's chivalric code, a code word for "patriarchal authority". It is his modus operandi, the "tricks" which he uses to "out-maneuver" the men, which reinforces the bond among men. The compelling metaphor of the "cloak" which he uses to impersonate both Octavio and DeMota is instructive. He even refers to "preliminary capework" in Aminta's seduction. When he seduces Isabella and Ana he wears the mantle of the men who pay allegiance to the moral order, but who ironically are only tricked by trying to operate outside this ordered life. Inside their cloaks, as inside their hearts, is Don Juan. Don Juan is a metaphor of their wish fulfilment. One sees each of the four women as representative of a type. The passive woman is Isabella.

> *A woman yes! That was my wrong,*
> *born to this privilege of debasement,*
> *Ordered to keep a civil tongue*
> *Locked in its civil ivory casement.*[49]

The obedient daughter Ana, who replies to the King of Castile who has given her in marriage to Don Juan:

> *Sir, its yours and my father's will.*[50]

The intellectual woman Tisbea:

> *Oh, Sir you know Homer?*[51]

And the wife Aminta who is also a social climber:

> *Then let my husband's will be done,*
> *Because God has blest me. I'm still*
> *A bride, but more: a royal one.*[52]

One thing they do have in common as far as Don Juan is concerned is that notwithstanding individual differences as women, any "Nobody can violate her." Ironically, Don Juan is the self-confessed "Nobody".

> *I'm nobody, that's all you know;*
> *My name is Nobody, or you're dead.*[53]

There is an interesting link between violence perpetuated against women and a fantasy of annihilating them, making them "nothing". Lemuel A. Johnson quotes Octavio Paz's Sons of La Malinche in the Labyrinth of Solitude. La Malinche, he says, is both victim and complicit, disturbance-generating wound:

> *It is true she gave herself voluntarily to the conquistador, but he forgot her as soon as her usefulness was over. She is "the very flesh of Indian woman" upon which the conquistador's chignon or macho rites and rights have left their mark and word, la Chingada. The idea of violence rules darkly over all the meanings of the word, and the dialectic of the "closed" and the "open", thus fulfils itself with almost ferocious precision. The chignon is the macho, the male, he rips open the chingada, the female, who is pure passivity, defenceless against exterior world." In the final analysis, "she loses her name;*

she is no one; she disappears into nothingness; she is nothingness." [54]

"Old World, New World. They're all one" says Juan.[55] Whether it is the medieval Knight or twentieth century conquistadors, the macho image of violence and power is played out on woman as rape. The passage of time has not significantly altered gender relations.

Don Juan's demise is predictable, not only is he mortal, but he has created too many enemies for himself. He is the enemy of the institutions of the society: state, Church and home. He has added murder to his seductions and his chase after chimeras leaves him an empty, unfulfilled man:

You see here a man born empty,
With a heart as heavy as yours;
There's no Hell you could offer me,
Sir, that equal to its horrors.[56]

What he seeks is not found in violating women but in agape, caring love. He forces his women victims to liberate themselves by becoming conscious of their powerlessness, facing up to their chains, to a new belief in their sovereignty:

Listen, Ana, don't you see
that what he's shown the lot of us
is that our lust for propriety
as wives is just as lecherous
as his? Our protestations
all marketable chastity?
Such tireless dedication's
almost holy! He set us free![57]

Octavio's desire to see Don Juan dead is rich with symbolism. He wishes to destroy within himself this fascination with rape and hopefully everyman's fascination, but this demands more than a negation, it demands an affirmation of the integrity of woman and a recognition of her as a sexually and intellectually empowered member of the human species. Walcott's imprint on the work is seen through his use of sexual imagery and the satirical, risqué, calypso genre. It is through these that the themes of sex as violence and the impotence of women are delineated. Let us examine these.

Don Juan sings:

Seville gave me the honor
of calling me Don Juan, the Joker,
and its true what I do may undo a
woman, but I renew her
and honor her with dishonour.[58]

This remarkable view of doing a woman a favour ("honor her with dishonour") when she is the recipient of unwanted sexual advances, is the reverse side of the coin, the suggestion that a woman welcomes the role of a raped victim:

Tell the stars over old Seville,
When we kill, we really don't kill.
Look, our swords are all sticks and our duels just stickplay
Sans humanité.[59]

The phallic images of "swords", "sticks", "stick play" are not to be seen as threatening. We really do not "kill" yet the refrain "sans humanité", which literally means "mercilessly", resonates with the desire to hurt, to wound. There is an interesting theory put forward by Elaine Scarry in "The Body in Pain, the making and unmaking of the world."[60] Lemuel A. Johnson, in commenting on this work, observes:

Scarry suggests, but does not, of course focus, in an island-in-between way (with its axe men and other architects of the vagina) on a form of woundability in which the female body is seen as essentially more woundable, or as "simply" and more "naturally" available for mis(use).[61]

It is with the intellectual Tisbea that Walcott's metaphors and images reach their wittiest heights, or lowest depths, depending on how one looks at it. It is rife with the double-entendres so fitting to the calypso genre. In response to Tisbea's "your metaphors they're pure Homer", [62] Hon Juan ridicules the notion that this woman must be taken seriously about metaphors, he can only respond to her in metaphors of sexuality. She becomes the temptress Eve:

The serpent stirs. Do you know the first metaphor of Eden Tisbea, the serpent? Do you know the winking one-eyed snake? Oh let us pray the serpent (are you Catholic, good) does not violate this sea-sprayed paradise; keep it down, like an eel, press this eel into its basket, sweet-salt fishergirl. We must be firm with it; here, put one hand firmly here, around its neck. That's right. Do you feel the monster, the devil, defying you? [63]

Images of sexual arousal abound in the phallic "serpent", "snake", "eel".

We note the use of the word "violate". Tisbea is simply a sexual object, so that the only "metaphors" that will be mixed are those of an aroused Don Juan and a not unwilling Tisbea in the grove.

In Catalinion's song, we are reminded that where there is sex, violence is not very far away:

That rod is the rod
of correction.[64]

And the fishergirl's song:

Tisbea went and bathe,
A swordfish take she maid.[65]

As liberated as Tisbea seems to be in her acceptance of her sexuality, she still is very conventional, she wants the respectability or stability of marriage. The mention of the word 'wife' find Don Juan reacting with uncharacteristic anger:

A wife? Well back to fig leaves!
A wife? You calculating bitch,
You're as heartless as the average
virgin back there! What privilege
comes from being Senor Tisbea?[66]

"You calculating bitch"! The violence is also verbal. No wonder Tisbea drowns herself. She is really for Don Juan simply a "bitch" once he has had her. She is nothing more or less. Such is the fate of the intellectual woman who dares to accept her sexuality in a macho world. One can hear the remarks about intellectual women coming from men who know that all she really needs to put her in her place is a man. This idea is often stated in more precise, explicit terms.

Ana's betrayal is contemplated by Don Juan thus:
Call of my trick? You must be sick, Sir!
Could I explain it to my prick, man?
Here comes Tenorio, your stickman!
Again we have to every virgin's grief
This tiger with a rose between its teeth.[67]

"Prick", "stickman", "virgin's grief", "tiger", "teeth" all attest to the woundability of woman on the one hand and the desire to inflict pain on the other. After her seduction, Ana at least is resolute in her need for revenge:

"Then kill him! Kill. . ." [68]

Don Juan's seduction of Aminta, the wife of Batricio introduces another dimension to the problematic relationship of macho man and victim-woman. He tempts her thus:

JUAN:	*You aren't below me, but that chance*
	Will come tonight. And not a beast.
	Rather a sacrificial lamb.
AMINTA:	*You think so? Do you hear me bleat?*
JUAN:	*A sacrificial lamb, one laid*
	not on an altar but a bed.
	revolving, slowly, on a sword.
	You blush easily.[69]

The metaphor of the victim is explicit here, as is the notion of woman's annihilation and torture: "Slowly on a sword". Don Juan weaves an awful web of deception to convince Batricio, her husband, that she is a "used woman". Poor Batricio! He, as everyman, rejects her thus:

I have no use for a used woman.
I have my honor and my pride.[70]

After this heinous conquest of the simple Aminta even Don Juan cannot feel pride in this:

I'm being ground down by my will.
These easy victories aren't fun anymore.[71]

Women are prey to be hunted, there is no fun in the chase if surrender is easy. Don Juan is at the end of his rampage on women. We will leave him to his fate for a while and listen to the women, to hear what they make of their fate as his victims. Isabella recognises women's status as property:

We'll sink like cattle to our knees
and thank that manipulator
of our stock price; after all, he's
royally found us a buyer,
a bit reduced, but their concern
is for negotiable meat,
and so I'm given back to Juan

honourably now, to be his mate.[72]

Aminta does not even remember his name.

She is too busy taking responsibility for her life:
...but I'm not leaving here without
at least a duke. I spent money
to get here.[73]

Ana has had her wish for revenge fulfilled, but beyond this resolution, this obedient daughter seems too mired in her role as mirroring "patriarchal authority" to find compassion for her father's murderer. Don Juan's death hopefully symbolises the demise of the desire to vicariously partake of a perception of woman as "woundable", as an acceptable receptacle of violence and compounding the insult by the belief that the victims enjoy this status. It should also alert us to the absence of love which is the corollary of this syndrome.

De Mota's observation on Don Juan is instructive:
There is no suffering more monstrous
than life without a center. Juan,
you have been loved by all of us
here, with a love you couldn't return.[74]

The Don Juan's of the world are incapable of love.

The raucous humour and sexually degrading images of women coupled with the obvious zest and uninhibited enjoyment with which Walcott fashions this musical, inclines one to believe that he is not unsympathetic to the vicarious titillation which Don Juan's escapades engender. Lemuel A. Johnson notes in discussing Walcott's "The Star Apple Kingdom":

As we reach conclusion in Walcott's poem of (re)membering we do become increasingly aware of a figure that haunts the phallocentric line of thought and its narration. The particulars of that figure's own history and identity are, however, very much overloaded by the foregrounded egocentricity of the male dreamer — until that is, "The Star Apple Kingdom" is, so to speak, held up against the light. When that happens attention is drawn to the way in which the female presence has all along been served up: "The woman's face, had a smile been decipherable/in that map of parchment so rivered with wrinkles/would have worn the same smile with which he now/cracked the day open and began his egg". The poem's lyrical and near solipsistic remembrance and transport now appear to have been powered by a typical Great Tradition traffic and trade in the female body. For example, it is obvious that the body is, for Walcott, the site of the wound which bore, and bears, historical consciousness. And it is just as clear that it does so in the appropriate mastering discourse.

The vision is in reality Pan-American, and common enough, being a form of speculation with the female in the course of which she becomes Land-in-Waiting and Virgin Continent which yield milk and honey – but only do so upon being ravished.[75]

The Joker of Seville bears the stigmata of this critique and leaves one to question whether Walcott conceives of woman as a temptation to disorder who deserves and contributes to her violation. This patriarchal view embedded in the Edenic myth is at the heart of Old Testament human consciousness. The other level of consciousness is the New Testament message of brotherhood/sisterhood of love and forgiveness. One would wish Walcott closer to this ideal in the portrayal of the problematic man/woman relationship. Of course, in the context of an experimental "musical" production one could only assume that much of the harshness of the rhetoric has been softened by the music, the speech and action!!

Psychological Plays

THE plays which have been selected for discussion can be seen as one text. The playwright seems to be obsessively working and reworking themes. One sees parallel concerns, in different forms. In a folkplay such as Dream and an experimental Broadway musical such as O'Babylon!, one notes in the former the Colonialist/African opposition while in the latter the Capitalist-Colonialist/African-Rastafarian opposition. Yet the strategy is the same since, essentially, Walcott is concerned with the creative process so that appropriation/hybridity/creolisation/syncrecity are all employed in opposition to a sterile limited view of history which refuses accommodation. The Last Carnival, The Joker of Seville, and O'Babylon! are obvious examples of this. The playwright's Adamic vision informs all his oeuvre. He has always believed that the New World offers a unique opportunity to be creative and to give things their names. This of course is the challenge of all post-colonial writers. Walcott sees the Robinson Crusoe/Castaway figure as a metaphor for this challenge to structure one's reality as he employs this theme in Pantomime. Yet all this experience exacts a cost. In the plays *Remembrance* (1980), *Pantomime* (1980) and *Franklin* (1989) the psychological cost is examined.

Frantz Fanon, French Antillean Psychologist from Martinique wrote extensively on the pathology of the Colonised in his text Black Skin, White Masks. He examines the paradox of the colonized, what he is and what people think he is. Mannoni, the Sociologist uses his research to produce the work Prospero and Caliban, subtitled the Psychology of Colonization using archetypes from Shakespeare's The Tempest to put into perspective the effects on the traumatized Blacks of the eighteenth and nineteenth centuries. The Imperialists' rampage into the world of Africa and Asia, pillaging and plundering people and products, and their arrogant assumption of superiority, was the occasion for this pathology.

For Shakespeare Caliban, the cannibal, the colonized would be taught language, but simply to curse with. He would be the hewer of wood and drawer of water. Manonni seeks to explain this relationship in psychological terms, in terms of this encounter between Prospero and Caliban, Coloniser and Colonised. One sees the convergence between post-colonial literature and a psychological extrapolation of this encounter in these plays. Post-colonial literature deals precisely with the creative possibilities of this encounter. One moves from Remembrance to Pantomime to Franklin in a movement from healing to health, from colonised man's rejection of self to mimicry of the coloniser, to acceptance of self via the process of appropriation/creolisation in Franklin. There is here a notion of transcendence, a vision of wholeness and of achievement, even through the vision might be superseded in the future by Walcott.

Edward Said, in propounding his thesis on culture as resistance and opposition, notes the many versions of The Tempest written by Latin American and Caribbean writers as a cultural effort to claim a restored and invigorated authority over the region. He observes that The Tempest is one of several fables that "stand guard" over the imagination of the New World, others are the adventures and discoveries of historical as well as fictional characters, such as Columbus, Robinson Crusoe, John Smith, and Pocahontas, and the adventures of Inkle and Yariko. He says:

> It is a measure of how embattled this matter of "Inaugural figures" has become that it is virtually impossible to say anything simple about any of them.[1]

The Tempest has been perhaps the most important text used to establish a paradigm for post-colonial readings of canonical works. It has now become the common practice in contemporary productions of the play to place some emphasis on colonialism. He observes:

> In fact, more important than the simple re-reading of the text itself by critics or in productions has been the widespread employment of the characters and structure of The Tempest as a general metaphor for imperial-margin relations (Manonni 1950; Dorsinville 1974) or, more widely to characterize some specific aspect of post-colonial reality.[2]

Mannoni's sociological work Prospero and Caliban: The Psychology of Colonialization, seeks to explain the process which moves man from native to "Colonized" or from European to Colonial. He states his intentions thus:

> If there is any merit in a psychological study it is because whereas we are accustomed to seeing a colonial situation as a case of the rich dominating the poor, the weak being

under the guardianship of the strong, of the systematic exploitation of a difference in standards of living and so forth, we are not in the habit of seeing it also as a case of the meeting of two entirely different types of personality and their reactions to each other, in consequence of which the native becomes "colonized" and the European becomes a colonial. These reactions are no doubt familiar enough in themselves, but they have never been properly analysed.[3]

Mannoni recognises the interplay of power, domination and the consequences on the human spirit. This is what makes the literature, which we term post-colonial, such a rich vein to explore. Fanon, the Psychiatrist and French "Colonized" Friedman perceive the challenge in this way:

Man is not merely a possibility of recapture, or of negation. If it is true that consciousness is a process of transcendence, we have to see too that this transcendence is haunted by problems of love and understanding. Man is a yes that vibrates to cosmic harmonies. Uprooted, pursued, baffled doomed to watch the dissolution of truths that he has worked out for himself one after another, he has to give up projecting unto the world an antinomy that co-exists with him.[4]

It is this paradox of the colonized, of what he is and what other people think he is — that is, what the colonizer defines him as — which he must stop projecting unto the world. It is this schizophrenia which the plays Remembrance (1980), Pantomime (1980) and Franklin (1989) are about.

George Lamming in Pleasures of Exile[5] suggests that Caliban is the excluded, that which is externally below possibility. He is seen as an occasion, a state of existence which can be appropriated and exploited to the purposes of another's own development. Both Lamming and Walcott seek to explode Prospero's old myth by Christening "language afresh", that is to show language as the product of human endeavour, until we make available to all the result of certain enterprises undertaken by men who are still regarded as the unfortunate descendants of people perceived of as languageless and deformed slaves.

Prospero's move outside society to the Pastoral, from the social to the natural, parallels the post-colonial concern with the replacing of culture and the renewal of the 'Adamic vision" of Walcott; where cultural and linguistic practices are exposed to radical and subversive change by their transportation to the New World. Prospero's experience in his New World certainly has that freshness of experience which Walcott stresses as characteristically post-colonial. It is Caliban who is most scrutinised. He can be interpreted in several ways. He is seen as aware of and accepting his mongrel past but not disabled thereby for future development; or else Caliban can shed his current servitude and physical disfigurements in the process of discovering his pre-colonial self. The latter Caliban is behind the nativist and other radical nationalisms like Garveyism and Rastafarianism. It is understandably more wholesome when Caliban sees his own history as an aspect of the history of all subjugated men and women, and comprehends the complex truth of his own situation.

Sylvia Wynter, Caribbean feminist, looks at one aspect of this "complex truth" of Caliban's social and historical situation as she ponders on the "absence of Caliban's woman as an alternative erotic model of desire".[6] This is particularly pertinent to the play Remembrance which celebrates, in the character of Albert Perez Jordan, the role of the colonial school master and his influence in reinforcing Imperialism's culture and the superiority of its canonical texts. His love for and enthusiastic enjoyment of learning and teaching laid the foundation for so much that is positive in colonial education. Yet the "antinomy that exists in him" prevents him from either genuinely loving himself or his "woman", thus his sexual and erotic model is his fantasy of European womanhood. His life takes on tragic proportions with the death of his radical son. The movement of change from Colonialism to Independence leaves many a colonial longing for his dependency and the good old days of living on the periphery of Empire.

Pantomime owes its conflict to the reversal of roles of that other "inaugural figure" Robinson Crusoe. Here Man Friday and Robinson Crusoe exchange roles with disconcerting consequences. This play as Said would suggest, must be seen, as

> ...not only an integral part of a political movement, but in many ways the movement's successfully guiding imagination, intellectual and figurative energy, reseeding and rethinking the terrain common to white and non-whites.[7]

Franklin is pure post-colonial discourse, which concerns itself with "place and displacement".

The dialectic of place and displacement is always a feature of post-colonial societies whether these have been created by a process of settlement, intervention or a mixture of the two. Beyond their historical and cultural differences, place, displacement and a pervasive concern with the myths of identity and authenticity is a feature common to all post-colonial literature in English.[8]

One cannot escape the importance of these concerns in Franklin if only because the play on the word "place" scintillates throughout the work and pits the diverse racial groups of the Caribbean against the Kiplingnesque Imperialist assumptions which both colonised and coloniser oftentimes consent to. Where is the place for these 'displaced' contenders? The play seeks to answer that question. Through the christening of language afresh Walcott moves these discourses from the margin to the centre of our literary canon.

REMEMBRANCE: A DISCOURSE OF THE ABSENCE OF CALIBAN'S WOMAN AS AN ALTERNATIVE SEXUAL EROTIC MODEL OF DESIRE, AS AN ALTERNATIVE SOURCE OF AN ALTERNATIVE SYSTEM OF MEANINGS

Remembrance is a celebration of the old colonial schoolmasters who delivered a colonial education based on the humanities and who contributed so much to the development of a cadre of well-read, well informed civil servants to replace the expatriates in the colonies. The play is as nostalgic as is Mr. Jordan, and the schoolmaster's nostalgia for the good old days of colonial rule, is palpable. Yet Remembrance is a counter-discursive play whose themes are post-colonial literature's standard fare, dependency, identity, home and the margin-centre interrogation of the hegemony of the imperial canon in literature.

What each of these literatures has in common beyond their special and distinctive regional characteristics is that they emerged in their present form out of the experience of colonization and asserted themselves by foregrounding the tension with the imperial power, and by emphasizing their differences from the assumptions of the imperial centre. It is this which makes them distinctively post-colonial.[10]

It has been noted that The Tempest has been the most important text used to establish a paradigm for post-colonial readings of canonical works; and the identification of the Prospero/Caliban nexus as a metaphor for imperial-margin relations. Said observes that:

The Cuban critic Roberto Fernandez Retamar makes the significant point that for modern Latin Americas and Caribbean, it is Caliban himself, and not Ariel, who is the main symbol of hybridity, with his strange and unpredictable mixture of attributes. This is truer to the Creole or mestizo composite of the new America.[11]

Said explains that Retamar's choice of Caliban over Ariel as symbol of hybridity is part of the ideological debate at the heart of the cultural effort to decolonize, to restore community and repossess culture, long after the political establishment of independent nations. Hybridity recognises value in all cultures. This serves to disturb the calculation of power and knowledge, producing gaps in what it all signifies. How does one read Jordan/Caliban, if we see him as a symbol of hybridity, as a symbol of one whose role as purveyor of culture, the dominant culture, and as one who is also a part of native culture? What meanings can we assume about his function in this post-colonial discourse?

The title of the play Remembrance is pregnant with meanings. There is the anniversary for Jordan's son's death, the seventh anniversary. This remains a painful remembrance, since his son's death, in the black power uprising, is an indictment of all Jordan stands for, the repudiation of all that he taught his students. The title reminds us also about the effects of Colonialism, especially the dependency syndrome. One reflects on and remembers Colonialism. Jordan's short story "Barrley and the Roof" explores these resonances. There are also memories of war, from a colonial's perspective, as one remembers the war in "My War Effort"; and the role of the Commonwealth contribution. The most compelling remembrance is of course the memories held of the class of colonial School masters of a particular period – pre-Independence – of whom Jordan is a fitting representative. This is a highly dramatic play which utilises shifts of time and flash-backs to create intense interest and tension. It also features a play within a play, "My War Effort": Probably the most startling feature of the play is the play with words, the shifts in registers of the language. The Caribbean is linguistically a polyglottic or polydialectal community, where a multitude of dialects inter-weave to form a generally comprehensible linguistic continuum. Thus, according to Ashcroft et al,

> the English language becomes a tool with which a "world" can be textually constructed. The most interesting feature of its use in post-colonial literature may be the way in which it also constructs difference, separation, and absence from the metropolitan norm. But the ground on which such construction is based is an abrogation of the essentialist assumptions of that form and a dismantling of its imperialist centralism.[12]

> Within the play itself and within the speech of each of its characters, there are displays of such a variety of English registers, that these may parallel the variety of English spoken throughout the British Commonwealth, and which differ from British English. This English of which post-colonial literature is composed, and the basis on which it is structured, undermines the assumption of British English as the norm, and other forms/ registers as exotic, different. Walcott's crafting of this English Language is a reflection of the sense of "newness" which he brings to the English of the New World – giving things their names – the "Adamic" vision. Jordan, who defines himself in the following excerpt,

is a striking example of this facility with the linguistic continuum – from dialect to British Standard English.

I would have written all this down, but that stubborn red ass, your editor, wouldn't hear. What about your eyes? He said. Before your memory goes, too, I'll send a boy over with a tape recorder, and if you can't write you could talk it out. Talk out what? I said. And he said, The story of your life, and I said, My life is nothing Ezra. I have been a damn fool, and besides, I said, I cannot write prose, Ezra. I am a poet, and he said, Everybody's eyes does dim a little as they get old, but as your eyes grow dim so your memories brighten, and if you can't write prose, at least you could talk it, and I told him. You got that from Molière, because I was a schoolmaster, you know. They called me One Jacket Jordan.

(Long Pause)

I was a school master. I was for a while Acting Principal Belmont Intermediate. They never appointed me. A school master

(Pause)

Who taught the wrong things.[13]

As Mr. Jordan drifts off into a recitation of Thomas Gray's "Elegy Written in a Country churchyard" one is struck by his self-effacement and his pedantry, his sense of regret, and his sense of futility. He taught "the wrong things". He is certainly not a British school master. His use of language marks him as different, separates him from and underscores his distance from the metropole. Does Gray's "Elegy" repeated by Jordan mean the same to him and his listeners as it does to the British School masters? We note this same phenomenon when Henri Christophe speaks. What Jordan says and how he says it must have meaning in the context of his relation to his history and his place as he exists on the margin of Empire. Acknowledging these calculations might supply unconscious significance in terms of power and knowledge. Jordan's identification with the dominant culture earns him the derision of his youthful "revolutionary" detractors.

Gray is ofay?, black is beautiful
Gray is shit
(chanting)
Jordan is a honky
Jordan is a honky
Jordan is a honky – donkey white nigger man![14]

This is deliberately culturally transgressive. It calls into question the old imperial norms. Gray is not accorded the canonization which Jordan accords him, the play on the word "Gray" to refer both to the poet and the colour, affords the linguistic shift to the colour "black" as "black is beautiful" and Jordan is rudely referred to as a "white nigger man" stressing his identification with the dominant culture. Jordan's response to this taunting is to remind anyone who wishes to think about it that:

> *"What is called poetry and art*
> *Colour don't matter! Colour don't matter!"* [15]

This interesting conundrum is certainly lost on his persecutors. Yet it may come back to haunt our consciousness when "Barrley on the Roof", a satire on independence, and "My War Effort", two of Jordan's best known short stories are examined. In reply to his interviewers who query whether these short stories draw on his own experience he says:

> *You could say it. If you prepared for libel. It is fiction. I always added a little truth*
> *to my stories. Peppersauce on the meat.* [16]

It is necessary to revisit the Prospero/Caliban nexus as a metaphor for imperial/margin relations in terms of the psychological consequences of this relationship. Prospero's "borrowed power", his magic, is really his unconscious need to use his imagination to people his world, but his "people" must be under his control. It is an ageless desire, it produces the archetypal being, whether an Ariel or a Caliban or a Man Friday. Psychologists see this syndrome in terms of pathology. It is the "lure of a world without men", a misanthropic melancholy, the need for solitude and isolation which permits one to people one's world with bogeymen and/or beautiful people. It is a substitute for dealing with the real world. The people in this imaginary world are all projections of the creator; they usually spring forth from feelings of guilt or shame, sexual guilt is high on the list. It is no wonder then that Prospero accuses Cailban of attempting to "violate the honour of his child". While this might be a projection of Prospero's sexual guilt, his own incestuous feelings towards his daughter Miranda, such a strong taboo cannot be accommodated and Caliban is a useful device in this regard. Caliban does however express his admiration of the lady, but makes a distressing comparison between her and his mother Sycorax:

> *And that most deeply to consider is*
> *The beauty of his daughter. He himself*
> *Calls her a nonpareil. I never saw a woman*

But only Sycorax my dam and she;
But she as far surpasseth Sycorax
As great'st does least.[17]

Caliban, in privileging Miranda over his mother Sycorax, also fulfils the need of the psychologically dependent person to venerate all that pertains to his master; his education, his cultural orientation are part and parcel of the dominant value system.

The Tempest is a prototype of colonial relationship. It is the education of the colonial for dependence, rather than freedom, that "Barrley on the Roof" is all about. It is linked to a colonial regulatory behaviour which defines "rational" in the context of an education which trains one not for freedom but for dependence. Caliban has been taught by Prospero how

To name the bigger light, and how the less,
That burn by day and night; and then I lov'd thee...[18]

When this love is betrayed by Prospero, Caliban's reaction to this betrayal is not to free himself from Prospero, but to find another form of dependence, another "foot to lick" as he says to Trinculo:

I'll show thee every fertile inch o' the' island,
And I will kiss thy foot. I prithee be my god.[19]

His notion of freedom is to have a new master; he rejoices in his ironic "freedom":

Ban, Ban, Ca-Caliban
Has a new master, get a new man.
freedom, high-day, freedom! freedom!
high-day freedom![20]

It is this ironic concept of freedom which Jordan tries to explore in his short story "Barrley on the Roof". Jordan's other son Frederick, paints an American flag on the roof. This is the latest manifestation in an American metamorphosis. His speech betrays this' he calls his father, "Pop", "Gee Pa", "What's up pop?" His father reminds him that they are in Trinidad:

Normal idiots might venture such exchanges as "Wha' happening daddy?" or "What it is Mammy do you?"[21]

Like Caliban he replaces one master for another and welcomes his role as "footlicker".

JORDAN: *I'm sorry, boy, I know what you painted. A symbol of distress. Help us*
             America! A cry from the Third World. Is that right Frederick?
FREDERICK: *Is just a flag on the roof Pa.*
JORDAN: *Well, it so happens that it's my roof and it's the American flag.*
FREDERICK: *You want me to make it the Union Jack*
JORDAN: *Bravo! It would at least be a monument to your father's values! It*
             would be something that he could look up to. Today art!
             Tomorrow turpentine.[22]

The son's signal of distress, "help us America", receives a ready response from the American Barrley:

When things get rocky and things get rough,
If the future looks like it might be tough,
If independence ain't what you expect,
Just call the United States, collect.[23]

Barrley wishes to buy the roof and ironically is refused by Frederick, whose art it is but whose roof it is not, though the father-owner suggests…

…Frederick, sell it. Is my house.
Sell it, or I cut off the grant from the Jordan
Foundation.[24]

Barley is very impressed by Frederick's display of integrity –

For what does it profit a man to gain
The whole world but to lose his own roof.[25]

Yet the son with all his "integrity" in not "selling out" is not very far removed from his father, as the Union Jack or the American flag are only symbols of their dependence. Their national flag, the symbol of their independence does not gain their allegiance. The interviewer notes, at the end of this enactment of the short-story, that a radical critic's view of Jordan's work is:

"…the defense of a man who has avoided the realities of our society and whose only
defense of his neglect lies in satire. We know nothing about the real Jordan, and had he
himself faced these problems, he might have been a more important writer. He has hidden
the truth behind a grinning mask that cares nothing for the sufferings of his black race."[26]

Ironically the critic believes that the writer "has avoided the realities of the society", while the writer is actually facing the reality of his society in a very intimate manner, he is facing up to the very real challenges of a dependency syndrome, which is symptomatic of post-colonial societies. The truth rather than being hidden is quite openly addressed. A critic who fails to detect the collective sufferings of "his black race" in Jordan's work, who believes that Jordan cares nothing for this suffering has not the imagination to comprehend Jordan's assimilation of the pain in order to produce the work. As Edward Said so incisively observes:

> *The post-imperial writers of the Third World therefore bear their past within them — as scars of humiliating wounds, an instigation for different practices, as potentially revised visions of the past tending toward a post-colonial future, as urgently reinterpretable and redeployable experiences, in which the formerly silent native speaks and acts on territory reclaimed as part of a general movement of resistance from the colonist.[27]*

While Jordan's apparent capitulation to the "colonist" culture rather than resistance to it may arouse derision, the pain is no less real. His wife is brutal in her frankness when she says:

> *…all the mockery and the way you talk like a black Englishman that he had to go out and do something.[28]*

This is a reference to their dead son and what motivated him to espouse the black radicalism that eventually took his life. However painful this observation is, it is a communal pain. Mr. Jordan cannot find the courage or comfort in making the ritual visit with his wife to his son's grave:

> *Is too much pain Mrs. Jordan. Too much. Don't make this a sad house, woman. Life marches on.[29]*

Sylvia Wynter, Caribbean feminist, notes that Western Europe's post-medieval expansion into the New World shifted its rationale for exploitation from the religious to behavioural regulation, thus the concept of the "non-rational inferior nature" of the people to be governed, was not seen in the male/female gender division but that between "men" and "natives". She contends that this shift from anatomical model of "sexual difference" as the referential model of mimetic ordering, to that of the physiognomic model of racial/cultural difference was no more powerfully enacted than in Shakespeare's play The Tempest. In the course of her incisive delineation of the meaning of this text, she raises the question of the absence of Caliban's woman thus:

> *This question is that of the most significant absence of all, that of Caliban's Woman, of Caliban's physiognomically complementary mate. For nowhere in Shakespeare's*

play and in its system of image-making, one which would be foundational to the emergence of the first form of a secular world system, our present Western world system, does Caliban's mate appear as an alternative sexual-erotic model of desire; as an alternative source of an alternative system of meanings. Rather there, on the New World island, as the only woman, Miranda and her mode of physiognomic being, defined by the philogenically "idealised" features of straight hair and thin lips is canonized as the "rational" object of desire; as the potential genitrix of a superior mode of human "life", that of "good natures" as contrasted with the ontologically absent potential genitrix — Caliban's mate — of another population of human, i.e., of a "vile race" "capable of all ill", which "any print of goodness will not take", a "race" then extra-humanly condemned by a particular mode of Original Sin deservedly "confirms them to a rock", thereby empowering the "race" of Miranda to expropriate the island, and to reduce Caliban to a labour — machine as the new "massa damnata" of purely sensory nature — "He does make our fire/fetch in our wood, and serve in offices/that profit us." [30]

Remembrance is also a discourse of the meaning of this absence, and the difference/deference to this absence/presence of Caliban's woman as erotic model of desire, is linked to a colonial regulatory behaviour which defines "rational" in the context of an education which not only trains one for dependence but for self-denigration and self-hatred. One notes the "system of image-making" in the portrayal of Mabel, wife of Jordan. Her appearance in nightdress, dressing gown, hat and boots, is as unsightly and uninviting a picture as can be. She is as unattractive in her speech as in her appearance. She is a member of the "vile race".

Is only now you come, you bitch. [31]

Her "earthy vulgarity" is referred to in contrast to her husband's teaching the children "diction", good English diction. Yet her role is that of nurturer, provider, messenger. She hurries out at four in the morning to an all night Bar and Grill to buy her husband hops and shark. She has burned out her talent in domesticity. She is the hymn-singing, Jesus-proclaiming "Nigger-mammy". She is the nurse who watches over the health of her family:

Albert, close the door eh?
Albert, you standing in a draft. [32]

Her Husband's response to her is the ironic:

Socrates had his Xantippe. Samson his Delilah and I have got Mabel. [33]

When she has had enough of this unromantic and unrewarding life and threatens to leave her husband, he speed her along thus:

Mistress Jordan! Do me a favour! Don't come back! [34]

Contrast this with the images and lyricism of "My War Effort" and its heroine Miss Esther Hope, as erotic a model of desire as one can hope, but it is quite obvious that the relationship portrayed is another form of dependence. It is an ironic relationship in which the Prospero figure is female. It comes as no surprise then that Jordan responds to Esther as "Sir" in this exchange. Where she questions him after he quotes King Henry V's famous war cry:

"Once more unto the breach, dear friends
Or close the wall up with our English dead!
In peace there's nothing so becomes a man
As modest stillness and humility;
But when the blast of war blows in our ears. . ."
Esther
What is this, Mr. Jordan?
Jordan
Sorry to appear in civvies, sir, but I simply
Couldn't find a spot to stash my gear.[35]

Just as Prospero/Esther not only represents the coloniser, but is endowed with the power to dominate through the "magic" of the division of the world into instinct/reason, non-rational native/rational coloniser. Jordan accepts this schema as Esther Hope becomes "Sir" precisely because she taught him language. He quotes Shakespeare, thus reinforcing the total identification of himself and his role with "our English dead", even when he is mouthing the words of an English King. To this extent Esther is the desired, erotic model, "the adorable Miss Esther Hope" to whom he proffers a rose. This adoration is not offended by being called an idiot;

When you call me an idiot, Miss Trout, I feel like a prince.[36]

Protestations of love are heard:

I love you, Esther. I love you and I'm afraid.[37]

This passion is not reciprocated by Esther Hope. Clearly the presence/ absence hierarchy vis-à-vis eroticism is reversed, as Jordan is not an erotic model for Esther. She brings the force and assumed superiority of her racial identity to bear on her attitude to his attentions:

> ...No more little games. I hate flirtations. We aren't a very frivolous race, the Brr...
> itish. So your little notes were very annoying. Not at all flattering.[38]

Yet she just may condescend to marry him, if he wants her to, but Jackson's silent cowardice puts an end to this magnanimous gesture of Esther's and she ponders on her possible rival. Caliban's woman gains him for among other reasons his own sense of inferiority, cowardice. Anna Hershel's appearance on the Jordans' doorstep functions to re-reinforce the absence/presence of Caliban's woman as erotic model of desire, all the emotional responses to Esther Hope of fiction are transferred to Anna Herschel. The consideration for her and her baby, the thoughtfulness captured in:

> I've gone around the house on velvet feet. I warned the sunlight entering her room
> not to make a noise. I wanted her to sleep after thirty five years of wandering among
> the ruins of bombed-out London. She said to me, last night, before she went to sleep,
> jokingly, "Maybe, I'll dance for you sometime," like Esther, Esther Trout? Believe me,
> Ezra, she is Esther Trout.[39]

Mabel has lived with her knowledge of her husband's preference for Miranda/Esther. She has lived with the knowledge of her absence from his purview of her as "erotic model":

> You think all I do is cook, sing hymns, and tolerate your moods. You think I don't
> read? You think I ain't realise who Padmore is? You think I never read "My War
> Effort" and realize that if you wasn't such a coward thirty years ago, you would of
> leave me? Well, the way I have watched you watching her, all I can see is memory and
> regret. Lord I ain't know why I had to come back for this.[40]

Her presence in his life would be, if belatedly acknowledged in a positive light, for "magnificence" not "Eros".

> I never been great enough to write about the simple things, about real magnificence,
> about you in fact, my dear.[41]

Mabel wants adoration and roses not magnificence:

> I ain't want no magnificence Albert...And to see that love in your eyes coming back
> again so fierce as if you wish you was young and could go away with her.[42]

That look is reserved not for her, but for Miranda/Esther/Anna. Caliban's sense of wonderment is expressed in:

> *...I never saw a woman*
> *But only Sycrorax my dam and she*
> *But she as far surpasseth Sycrorax*
> *As greatest does least.*[43]

precludes this. To Jordan is given the last word and there is a more positive assessment of his life as he speaks to the interviewer for the last time:

> *I taught those little bastards well, didn't I? I taught with a passion. Wrong things or not. Some of them are big shots today, Judges. But I was a holy terror in that classroom, boy Pilly. There would be a deathly silence when I entered, the kind of silence that we keep for kings. I taught them with the love that comes through books and I inspired the fear that would give them confidence...*
>
> *I am trying to tell all you blasted young whippersnappers that Thomas Gray is saying: It doesn't matter where you're born, how obscure you are, that fame and fortune are contained within you. Your body is the earth in which it springs and dies. And it's the humble people of the world, you Jones, you Walcott, and you Brown and you Fonesca, and you Mango Head, that he's concerned about. And he's concerned about them from the very first verse of his "Elegy" as he meditates aloud. Now, class, close books and recite from memory!* [44]

Jordan is undeniably a symbol of great inspiration to those whose lives he influenced. He is an unrepentant anglophile, who fearlessly embraces the Imperial canons, and is the "good" subject in Michel Pêcheux's sense of the term as he investigates the creation of subjects through ideological practices:

> *He (Pecheux) argues that there are three modes in which subjects are constructed. The first mode is that of "Good" subjects who result from Identification; they "freely consent" (in Althusser's terms) to the discursive formation which determines them.*[45]

Jordan's identification with Imperial culture is absolute. Walcott's play Remembrance drags the entire post-colonial discourse on hybridity and creolisation, identity, dependence, to the forefront and disturbs the calculation of power and knowledge which the imperial centre claims.

PANTOMIME: A Discourse on Creolisation, Language and the Mimetic Journey from Periphery to Centre

Pantomime is a crystalisation of Walcott's philosophy on creolisation and language. Here, in the satiric mode, he hones his skills and beliefs about the value of the embrace "of the past and present, between imperializer and imperialised, between culture and imperialism" not to level or reduce differences, but rather to convey the sense of the interdependence between things. The re-interprets and redeploys experiences in which the former silent native speaks out and acts on territory "reclaimed as part of a general movement of resistance from the colonist". His New World "Adamic Vision" of giving things their names is hilariously mimed by Jackson in all its inconsistent confidence. "Language is ideas" he intones pompously. It is the Cariobbean's and Walcott's good fortune that so varied a field of "lects" is available for use. The neologisms of Trinidadian speech are liberally sprinkled throughout the play, words like "rake" in "your come back with that same rake again?", "Bohbolee", "mamaguy". It is suggested that the tropes of post-colonial text may be read as metonymy, that language variance is metonymic of cultural difference:

> ...While the tropes of post-colonial text may be fruitfully read as metonymy, language variance itself in such a text is far more profoundly metonymic of cultural difference. The variance itself becomes the metonym, the part which stands for the whole. That "overlap" of language which occurs when texture, sound, rhythm, and words are carried over from the mother tongue to the adopted literary form, or when the appropriated English is adapted to a new situation, is something which the writer may take as evidence of his ethnographic or differentiating function – an insertion of the "truth" of culture into the text (sometimes conceived as an insertion of its essential cultural purity). Technical devices used by writers who come from an oral society (one with no tradition of writing) for instance, can be mistaken for "power words", "power syntax", and "power rhythms" which reproduce the culture by some process of embodiment.[46]

Nothing so separates Englishman Harry Trewe from Trinidadian Jackson Phillip as his use of the English language. The difference between Harry Trewe's English and Jackson Phillip's is particularly noticeable in the texture, sound and rhythm, the metaphors which Jackson employs. This is particularly noticeable in Jackson's calypsos, and his derisive critique of "Music Hall" language and sentimentality:

> "O silent sea, O wondrous sunset," and all that shit. No. He shipwrecked. He desperate, he hungry. He look up and he see this fucking goat with its fucking beard watching him and smiling, this goat with its forked fucking beard and square yellow eye just like the fucking devil, standing there...

> (pantomime's the goat and Crusoe in turn)

Smiling at him and putting out its tongue and letting go one fucking bleeeeeh! And Robbie ent thinking bout his wife and son and O silent sea and O wondrous sunset; no, Robbie is the First true Creole, so he watching the goat with his eyes narrow, narrow, and he say: blehhh, eh? You muther-fucker, I go show you blehhh in your goat-ass, and vam vam, next thing is Robbie and the goat, mano a mano, man to man, man to goat, goat to man, wrestling on the sand, and next thing we know we hearing one last faint, feeble bleeeeeehhhhhhhhhhhhh, and Robbie is next seen walking up the beach with a goatskin hat and a goatskin umbrella feeling like a million dollars because he have faith! [47]

This tour-de-force, is creative, energetic and rhythmic. While it is deliberately transgressive culturally, it serves to emphasise not only difference in the use of language, but in the power which resides in language itself. Moreover, the theme of culture as conflict and struggle and the energy which this produces is the essence of Creole, the "First True Creole" whether as native or as actor or as concept. It is "guerrilla warfare":

> *The transgressive, invasive structure of the black "national" text, which thrives on rhetorical strategies of hybridity, deformation, masking and inversion, is developed through an extended analogy with guerrilla warfare that became a way of life for the maroon communities of runaway slaves and fugitives who lived dangerously, and insubordinately.* [48]

The relations of discourse are of the nature of warfare, in which if one expects to survive one must take maximum advantage of local environments, of what is given, striking and withdrawing with great rapidity, trying to catch one's adversaries in cross-fire, choosing one's battles carefully. These strategies are well employed by Jackson in his struggle for psychic survival and wholeness. Pantomime is, quintessentially, a joyous celebration of language and the many uses to which it is put. This concern is exploited and delineated in the form of a counter-discursive play, which comments on the historical and personal conflicts that have dominated life in the Caribbean. In doing so Walcott uses one of the "inaugural figures" who stands guard over the imagination of the New World, Robinson Crusoe. In a nutshell, Harry Trewe, Englishman and owner of the Castaway Guest House is a retired actor, while his general factotum, Jackson Phillip, Trinidadian is a retired calypsonian. The action of the play takes place in a gazebo on the edge of a cliff, on the island of Tobago. Harry Trewe wishes to entertain his guests with a pantomime he co-authored, called "Robinson Crusoe", he wants Jackson to play Man Friday. Jackson will have none of it. The roles are reversed so that Jackson can play Robinson Crusoe and Harry Trewe, Man Friday. This reversal of roles, white Englishman playing Man

Friday, servant, while black Trinidadian plays Robinson Crusoe, generates paradoxes in which black Trinidadian interrogates and deconstructs Imperial assumptions. Pantomime examines the relationship between the colonizer and the colonized. Mannonni's insights into this relationship are worth examination. He notes that Daniel Defoe's, Robinson Crusoe recounts the long and difficult case of a misantrophic neurosis. His hero, who is at odds with his environment, gradually recovers psychological health in solitude. He comes to accept the presence of creatures upon whom he tries to project the image – at once terrifying and reassuring of "another". Then he has a friend, "dumb" at first, like his parrot. The "dumb" friend is his Man Friday, so that the first reversal one notes in the play Pantomime, is that Man Friday is not dumb, he speaks, and speaks combatively. Mannoni notes that some of the semi-human creatures the unconscious creates, such as Caliban or the Lilliputian, or Man Friday, reveal their creator's desire to denigrate the whole of mankind. Defoe saw Robinson Crusoe as himself, and Mannoni states:

> The "case" of Defoe, then, broadly, is one of misanthropy, melancholy, a pathological need for solitude, the projection of his faults on to others, a sense of guilt toward his father, repressed affection for a daughter whose sex he preferred to ignore... Thence emerged the story of Robinson, in the way a dream might occur. When this dream was published, however, all Europe realized that he had been dreaming it. For more than a century afterwards the European concept of the savage came no nearer reality than Defoe's representation of him, and it was on that figure that the European, if he was more or less infantile in character or, like Rousseau, unable to adapt himself to reality, projected the inner image of which there was no counterpart in the solid and too familiar world of reality.[49]

Imperialism thus structured its concept of the native on a projection of a construct of "savage" which natives accepted and mimed unquestionably for centuries. It could only have happened through conquest, the harnessing and exploitation of resources, physical, cultural and propagandistic, to reinforce its dominance on the native psyche. The struggle for power now resides in the post-colonial writer's dominance of language, created anew, to reverse the psychological handicap of centuries. Jackson is a worthy combatant in the struggle to wrest power from Harry's imperial assumptions about himself, which Jackson undermines. It is very clear that words, expressions or propositions change their meaning according to the positions held by those who use them – that is, they find their meaning by reference to these positions. It is this feature which will lend pungency to what Jackson says. If he is not Man Friday, he rejects this notion of being a cannibal/Caliban, he is Robinson Crusoe, imperialist and has the power to impose his culture on Man Friday/Harry. This becomes pungent humour:

> HARRY: *Friday, you bring Crusoe, me, breakfast now. Crusoe hungry.*
> JACKSON: *Mr. Trewe, you come back with that rake again? I tell you I ain't no actor, and I ain't walking in front a set of tourists naked playing cannibal. Carnival, but not canni-bal.*[50]

Jackson's language bears the burden of his experience as a conscious native, who well understands the Imperial "text". He would neither tolerate denigration from Harry nor from his parrot from a "pre-colonial epoch". Harry's rejoinder that it is a "creole parrot" because of its accent, serves to foreground the notion of the mimetic, albeit a creative mimicry. Jackson's tolerance of past resonances "Heinegger, Heineeger", of Nazism will prove to be very low. While language can be mimicked, it can also be used as a tool of empowerment. Jackson's story about the use of the "ice pick" to silence the Indian fellows "want to play nigger" is as much about violence as it is about power. So is Harry's story about "a wrench this big". It is a form of whistling in the dark. It is the language that interrogates the cultural norms of religion and education which have controlled the colonized and which startles by its logic.

> JACKSON: *Hilarious, Mr. Trewe? Supposing I wasn't a waiter, and instead of breakfast I was serving you communion, this Sunday morning on this tropical island, and I turn to you, Friday, to teach you my faith, and I tell you kneel down and eat this man. Well, kneel nuh! What you think you would say, eh?*
> *(Pause)*
> *You, this white savage?*
> HARRY: *No, that's cannibalism*
> JACKSON: *Is no more cannibalism than to eat a god. Suppose I make you tell me: For three hundred years I have made you my servant. For three hundred years...*
> HARRY: *It's a pantomime, Jackson, just keep it light...Make them laugh.*
> JACKSON: *Okay*
> *(Giggling)*
> *For three hundred years I served you breakfast in...in my white jacket on a white veranda, boss, bwana, effendi, baccra, sahib...that was my pantomime. Every movement you made, your shadow copied...*
> *(stops giggling)*

And you smiled at me as a child does smile at his shadow's helpless obedience,
boss, bwana, effendi, baccra, sahib. Mr. Crusoe. Now. . .

HARRY: Now?

(Jackson's speech is enacted in a trance-like drone, a zombie)

JACKSON: *But after a while the child does get frighten of the shadow he make. He say*
to himself, That is too much obedience, I better hads stop. But the shadow
don't stop, no matter if the child stop playing pantomime, and the shadow does
follow the child everywhere; when he praying the shadow pray too, when he
turn round frighten, the shadow turn round too, when he hide under the sheet,
the shadow hiding too. He cannot get rid of it, no matter what, and that is the
power and the black magic of the shadow, boss, bwana, effendi, baccra, sahib,
until it is the shadow that start dominating the child, it is the servant that start
dominating the master. . .
(laughs maniacally, like The Shadow)
And that is the victory of the shadow, boss.
(Normally)
And that is why all them Pakistani and West Indians in England, all them
immigrant Fridays driving all you so crazy. And they go keep driving you till
you go mad. In that sun that never set, they's your shadow, you can't shake
them off.[51]

Imperialism is a two-edged sword, the dominated become dominant,
the mimics become co-creators, the peripheral becomes central, and it is
done through the power of the word. Sometimes, in the "naming" of the
new found power there is an element of madness, as in the separatist, nativist
movements, and the language, the voice, the word makes no sense, becomes
eccentric. It is difficult to call anything by the same name twice:

JACKSON: *(inventing language) Amaka nobo sakamaka khaki pants kamaluma Jesus*
Christ! Jesus Christ kamalogo!
(Pause. Then with a violent gesture)
Kamalongo kaba!
(Meaning: Jesus is dead)[52]

Words like "patamba", "Rogoongo! Rogoongo", "Backaraka
Backaraka", "Banda Karan!" "Zohgooooor!" Whose meanings range from
camera, to table, cup, floor, are arbitrary signs. Language is a living vital
human behaviour, it grows out of other languages, there is no need to start
from scratch, one simply has to:

...seize the language, replace it in specific cultural location, and yet maintain the integrity of that Otherness, which historically has been employed to keep the post-colonial at the margins of power, of "authenticity" and even of reality itself. [53]

Jackson is going to play Robinson Crusoe "my way", he is "meticulous", he is a stickler for detail. If he is going to do this, it must be done with integrity. No detail is to be left out. He takes his role seriously, so seriously that Harry is afraid that he is about to "commit Art". He calls the project off. This is manifestly an Imperial ploy, shades of Froude, the natives are getting ambitious, they are now casting their eyes at leadership of the colonies, this must be stopped:

I for myself, look upon Trinidad and the West Indies generally as an opportunity for the further extension of the influence of the English race in their special capacity of leadership and governors of men. We cannot with honour divest ourselves of our responsibility for the blacks, or after the eloquence we have poured out and the self-laudation which we have allowed ourselves for the suppression of slavery, leave them now to relapse into a state from which slavery itself was the first step of emancipation. Our world-wide dominion will not be of any long endurance if we consider that we have discharged our full duty to our fellow-subjects when we have set them free to follow their own devices. If that is to be all, the sooner it vanishes into history the better for us and for the world. [54]

It is fortunate the J. J. Thomas was there to remind us that Froude was referring to people like Jackson, people who were ready to be leaders, "to commit Art", people who were "embellishers and improvers". J. J. Thomas thunders:

But our opinion is equally decided that Mr. Froude has transgressed the bounds of decent political antagonism, nay, even of commonsense. When he presumes to state that it was not for any other object than the large salaries of the Crown appointments, which they covet for themselves that the reform leaders are contending. This is not criticism it is slander. [55]

So is Harry's plea to stop the show slanderous – to wish to suggest to Jackson that he is taking things "too seriously" and that in effect one can just simply revert to business as usual. Once more Harry becomes master and Jackson servant "take away the breakfast things". Jackson reaffirms his independence:

...here I am getting into my part and you object. This is the story...this is history. This moment that we are now acting here is a history of imperialism; it's nothing less than that. [56]

Harry is beginning to comprehend the full significance of Jackson's improvisation, he will have to learn or reassess his own assumptions about the nature of things.

> HARRY: *All right, so it's Thursday. He comes across this naked white cannibal called Thursday, you know. And then look at what would happen. He would have to start to... well, he'd have to, sorry... This cannibal, who is a Christian would have to start unlearning his Christianity. He would have to be taught... I mean... he'd have to be taught by this African... that everything was wrong, that what he was doing... I mean, for nearly two thousand years... was wrong That his civilization, his culture, his whatever, was... horrible. Was all... wrong. Barbarous, I mean, you know. And Crusoe would then have to teach him things like, you know, about... Africa, his gods, patamba, and so on... and it would get very very complicated and I suppose ultimately it would be very boring, and what we'd have on our hands would be... would be a play and not a little pantomime...* [57]

This would take a quite profound transformation for Thursday, Man Friday and Robinson Crusoe, an achievement devoutly to be wished for. It is the psychological health of Harry Trewe/Robinson Crusoe which Jackson with his probing and compassion will restore, for like Defoe/Crusoe, Harry Trewe is a lonely, melancholy man. Mannoni asserts that the rationale for the Robinson Crusoe personality type is guilt and the need for punishment.

> *...the hero has to face either the perils of the miseries of exile; they are either punishments or, as it were, scarecrows, the two ideas being easily linked in that of prohibition.* [58]

These are, for Mannoni, victims of a "misanthropic neurosis" who seek exile, with all its miseries, as either punishments for perceived prohibitions from childhood, or as bad creatures on whom the child projects his own desire to be naughty and the parents who forbid him to be naughty. All these are unconscious urges which can be painfully unearthed. Jackson takes on the role of psychologist who helps Harry to face up to his unconscious urges for punishment, for exile. To do this Harry must give up his need to "denigrate" other human beings, to project unto others negativity. He must accept equality among human beings, "man to man" relationships. In showing Jackson the script he had written for the pantomime, there is "man to man" friendly ribbing about the script. It is in parts a very macho in-house type of ribaldry, the "pee-break" episode must have special resonances for men. There is equality in "natural functions" but no equality status, where people perform these functions, separates them, marks them as different, "out-house" or "guest house". This is the prelude to the death of the parrot, which Jackson, as Friday pretends to mimic. The savage says:

Me na strangle him, bwana. Him choke from prejudice.[59]

Jackson and Harry go through an elaborate pantomime in which they transmute the violence of their encounter, the master/servant encounter, by recognising each other's innate kindness and compassion. Harry empties himself of his suppressed rage and anger for his wife whose superior talents he admits to, and in so doing he recognises that an "Albatross" has fallen from his neck, he is free of his "neurosis".

The play ends as it began with the exuberant play on words "goat to pack", "goat to bed", "Egoat-istical" as Jackson goes back to his "gift that's my God-given calling", his gift of words as a calypsonian:

Well, a limey name Trewe came to Tobago.
He was in show business but he had no show,
So in desperation he turn to me
And said: "Mr. Phillip" is the two o' we,
One classical actor and one Creole,
Let we act together with we heart and soul.
It go be man to man, and we go do it fine,
And we go give it the title of pantomime.
La da deed a da da
Dee da da da da da da...[60]

Creolisation come through the use of the "imperial" language with which Walcott is familiar, and the faith (which is an absolute given for the Creole actor/writer) in the creative power of appropriation. This is the faith that knows that identity is not given and eternally determined, neither is privileged status something total and complete of itself, whether it be Imperial canons or "master styles", but that transformation is always possible through creative mimesis.

FRANKLIN: A TALE OF THE ISLANDS : "PLACE" AND MIS-PLACED LOVE ON THE FRINGES OF A DYING EMPIRE

It does seem self-evident that the very nature of colonisation implies places to be colonised, displacement of peoples and the physical and psychological consequences of this disruption. It is also seemingly self-evident that post-colonial literature would concern itself with this rich vein of thematic material.

A major feature of post-colonial literatures is the concern with place and dis-placement. It is here that the special post-colonial crisis of identity comes into being; the concern with the development or recovery of an effective identifying relationship between self and place. Indeed, critics such as D. E. S. Maxwell have made this the defining model of post-coloniality. A valid and active sense of self may have been eroded by dislocation, resulting from migration, the experience of enslavement, transportation, or "voluntary" removal for indentured labour. Or it may have been destroyed by cultural denigration, the conscious and unconscious oppression of the indigenous personality and culture by a supposedly superior racial or cultural model. [61]

The play Franklin is an exploration of the erosion of this sense of self which displacement symbolises in a search for "place", for "home". One of the most interesting observations one can make about Franklin is the frequency with which the word "place" occurs, and the different levels of meaning of the word in the context in which it is used. Not only is the word "place" filled with many resonances, but words and phrases indicating "place" also tingle with concepts which clarify meaning in the play. "Place" actually functions inter alia as space, locality, rank, office, cultural place, metaphor and psychological place. What do these meanings indicate? Certainly they indicate the extent to which the theme of identity is explored in the play. Love is another theme which is delineated in the play. It is placed/misplaced, equated with possession, power, manipulation. Love is also seen as loyalty and sacrifice. It is misplaced, disassociated from respect or human dignity. These themes are forged against the evanescent "green flash" of a dying empire.

The symbolic "green flash" which Franklin gambles against seeing at sunset, registers human transitoriness, the transitory nature of all things, the need to hold on to the desires which elude him, which are just out of reach. It is the lure of security which is manifested in one man as envy. It is seen in Ramsingh who gives his child an English name.

> I gave you an English name, because
> I was ashamed and full of envy. For that
> I also curse myself. [62]

There is also the envy of the departing "captains and kings" like Willoughby, who in preparing to return to "Mr. Atlee's England" somewhere in Dorset, cannot help but envy Ramsingh, who remains in the beautiful tropical island:

> *That's right. Keep grinning, Pundit, nice revenge.*
> *Back to the Welfare allotments, free dental care,*
> *the immigrants on the dole, lots of your people,*
> *the absolute grey monotony of it all.*[63]

The "grey monotony of it all" is a fitting contrast to the beauty of the islands as Franklin describes it:

> *Look at the light now. Soft and grey as England.*
> *Look at that light. An empire dying. Spectacular.*
> *How can a view I've known for seventeen years*
> *repeat my astonishment more than any woman?*
> *It's all mine. Every fertile inch of it.*[64]

This "place" which Franklin claims as his, is his by virtue of British Imperial conquest. The Rastafarians in O'Babylon! see their 'place' as in Africa, because of the Imperial plunder and slave trade. Franklin and the Rastafarians are therefore linked by a mutual sense of place/displacement. Rudyard Kipling, poet par excellence of British imperialism, is very much alive in the hymn "Recessional" which Methodist Minister Pritchett has his congregation sing weekly. The memory/melody runs throughout the play, the Gotterdammerung of which they sing is seen as a warning for those who may not have "a humble and a contrite heart". Franklin for example, is one such, whose Achilles heel is to confuse pride of possession with "love" and to make objects of people. He gains no insight into his error, after yet another betrayal, when he says

> *...And I want you to listen Cook*
> *to treachery. Something in me must cause it.*
> *There must be some bloody seal-FOOL!*
> *On this forehead!* [65]

This is said in response to a perceived betrayal by his protégé Clive Morris, who is now fraternizing with his political "enemies". This is before the knowledge of the most painful betrayal by the same Clive Morris in impregnating Maria. His former wife was also unfaithful to him with Willoughby. Does he realise what in him "causes" it? Willoughby tries to explain it to him:

> *You're so arrogant with your damned humility,*
> *You dispense justice with the scales of your eyes*
> *swaying the way you want them, and when they settle*
> *they do so on the level that you want them.*
> *And everything else hangs on their balance.*
> *You look down on us, Luther. You think I'm coarse.*
> *You put a distance between those you love,*
> *as if love was another judgement. Amy knew this.*
> *And too much power ends in impotence.*
> *And that's why she turned to me, for friendship,*
> *for someone coarse and ordinary, not an idiot*
> *wrapped up in his own legend. And that one there,*
> *it'll happen to her. Because you invite it.*
> *You want to be wounded, so your pride can win.*
> *So you can dispense forgiveness, well, friend*
> *damn your forgiveness. There, look at that smile.*
> *It's so bloody superior. So removed.*
> *Above it all, correct?* [66]
> *Reverend Pritchett "places" him well when he says:*
> *Do you know why we keep singing the Recessional?*
> *I see everything in you that was wrong with the empire.*
> *I just pray I don't repeat the same mistakes.*[67]

Yet it is to those whom Franklin "looks down on" that one must turn for definitions of place. When Cook responds to Maria's concerns about the negative attitude of the village towards her, now that she lives in Franklin's house, (and particularly the attitude of the Postmistress who looks "right through me") Cook says:

> *Man is her problem, not the Post.*
> *By which I mean the Post office. I don't play.*
> *I work here twenty-five years, twenty-five years*
> *with Mr. De La Grenade, then with Captain Franklin.*
> *Shadows cross like leaves across my eyes.*
> *So I can't take no waste of time from a postmistress.*
> *Life too short for that. So find yourself.*
> *Accept yourself. Carry your race with pride.*[68]

Cook is making the valid point that the psychological "place" everyman needs is not found in space, location, status or office. It is found in self-acceptance. In self respect. Identity resides in self-discovery. This is the central message of the play, all the other characters and situations will help to shed light on this message.

It is Charbon, (Moses Goodnight) the fisherman who expresses grievance and a keen sense of disinheritance and loss, who believes that Franklin has stolen the de La Granade property from him, by altering the deed. Charbon believes that his sentence to prison "for threatening and for trespass" stems from the fact that

> ...*they say La Granade not of sound mind*
> *Because he will his property to a nigger.*[69]

Charbon, whose sense of disinheritance is a metaphor for the colonial state, opines:

> ...*so if this wasn't my land then where is it?*
> *Africa? I lose Africa. Franklin still have England. But for him to have both here and England while all I had was love, that was them justice.*[70]

His aggrieved sense of dispossession, reminds us that for all those who lived the colonial experience, colonizer or colonized, a sense of self may have been eroded by dislocation. This sense of dislocation results from migration, the experience of enslavement, transportation or indenture. This dialectic of place and displacement is a feature of post-colonial literature.

> *No, but because a nigger must know his place!*
> *He must know his people. They will never make him captain...*[71]

In trying to circumscribe Morris' destiny by the suggestion that somebody will or will not "make him captain", he seeks to devalue and negate Morris' intelligence and abilities, he is unable to perceive Clive Morris in all the fullness of his humanity, as someone who can be motivated by ambition to achieve whatever he sets out to achieve given the opportunity to do so. In trying to 'place' Morris in some category called "nigger', a man like himself, Charbon limits his life to one of self-hatred and sterility. He needs his hatred to justify his limitations, to justify his exclusion from the community of men of goodwill. He thus remains a marginal figure, which Willoughby's description fits;

> *Charbon's Their big boo-boo and obeah man,*
> *Their new witch doctor!*[72]

Ramsingh's version of "place" is fatalistic. He says to his daughter whom he visits at Franklin's house:

> *You never knew your place. To find one's place. To be content with how the world divided, that is peace. I do not like to see my child unhappy.*[73]

This is of course ironic, since Ramsingh has confessed to not being content with "how the world divided", he gives his Indian children English, not Indian names. Does this show contentment? If Maria does not "know her place", it is because her father has already implanted within her a discontentment with who she is – an Indian girl from Coolie Village; this alienation of vision and crisis in self-image is a function of displacement, it is the cause of the schizophrenia which affects both Ramsingh and his daughter and which undermines the "self acceptance" which Cook privileges above everything else. Ramsingh's fatalism, his sense of powerlessness are very real consequences of oppression, Ashcroft et al, in The Empire Writes Back, remind us that:

> *In postcolonial societies, the participants are frozen into a hierarchical relationship in which the oppressed is locked into position by the assumed moral superiority of the dominant group; a superiority which is reinforced when necessary by the use of physical force.*[74]

Nonetheless, Ramsingh's fatalism is a deterrent to growth and fulfilment, it denies him a sense of self–respect and self-worth. As an individual he is left with nothing more than the consolation of chastising the fates rather than loving his innate abilities. Yet Ramsingh understands the role of culture in determining 'place'. In explaining the discontinuance of his Hindi-teaching School he says:

> *All the boys look up in my face*
> *I saw for the first time. They were not Indian boys...*
> *They were, well, West Indian, we are a small community,*
> *And I said to myself, suddenly... of what use is it?*
> *In a few years, our language will be dead.*
> *It cannot suffer transplantation... so I have pulled it up,*
> *And something else will grow.*
> *Perhaps our religion will die... some of our customs are dead.*[75]

There is no place he believes for teaching the Hindi language to West Indian boys, since not only is it isolating these boys, but denying the reality of a society which is not Indian but West Indian. There is obvious ambivalence in this attitude. What prevents English-speaking East/West Indians from learning Hindi? Why should they learn French, Latin, or Spanish and not Hindi or Swahili for that matter? Would denying them a tool to communicate with others of this language group make them any less West Indian or any more self-accepting? There is something as negative in this stance as the fatalism of 'knowing' one's 'place'. Instead of limiting one's options, one should expand them, as one expands one's possibilities and embraces diversity, one opens up spaces for one's "place" in which one may feel "at home".

Ironically, while Ramsingh is giving up teaching Hindi, he holds on to his Indian customs and traditions and recognises the value of having these. He contends that:

> ...I have tried to keep some of the customs
> some of the formalities, especially of religion,
> otherwise without that a race is nothing.
> I was not always successful.[76]

The psychological value of accretion is very clear to Ramsingh. "A race is nothing" without the acceptance of one's culture. He administers the "teeluck" to Franklin noting that:

> ...It is the dying of India in another
> country that I do here, but I know you gentlemen does
> keep a little piece of Britain, in your heart.[77]

This incorporation of India in the "heart" provides the telling indictment Ramsingh makes against the descendants of Africa for not keeping Africa in the "heart' when he says:

> They are not like us, because we have a memory
> of certain things, our customs, history, our religion.
> We have no slavery to be ashamed of.
> That is why it is hard to control them.[78]

While Ramsingh does not so state, his Indian presence in the West Indies is due not to slavery but to indenture, a more benign state of exploitation than slavery and one which since it respected the family unit and customs of the indentured, left these intact, in a New World setting, providing the psychological advantage to which Ramsingh refers. Thus in the pecking order of 'place' as status, Ramsingh pays obeisance to the "English" as definitely at the top of the pile, as the dominant power, and "they" who are "not like us", meaning the African masses, at the bottom. This does not help Ramsingh though, because Cook's definition still stands the test of scrutiny. Does he accept himself? Or is he forever looking up to Franklin and his ilk? Maria accuses her father of hypocrisy because she understands the shame she has brought upon him by living with the Englishman Franklin. She understands his hatred of the man, and is hurt that because of his own feelings of inferiority he cannot express these emotions to Franklin but rather fawns on him. This behaviour is a well documented survival strategy in master/slave relationships:

> ...*How you think I feel to see you out*
> *there among white men, with sahib this,*
> *and sahib that, and in your heart you burning*
> *up with shame? Yet you still doing it, you*
> *still doing it. How am I different?* [79]

Cook is justifying the "licks" which she gave to her nephew Clive Morris in order to teach him "to respect God, and your place in life", to be a "respectful black man", arouses his ire as he tries to define his "place" in life thus:

> *Is that what you mean. "My place in life."*
> *My place in life is there on the sea.*
> *You know what? When I touch land, when I see*
> *This house, I feel to vomit, I get sick!*
> *You all make me sick! That is my place in life,*
> *There, where I can be myself, without woman, child,*
> *Captain, aunt, without a name. No name!*
> *Nothing to sign. Just sea!*
> *You forget on the sea.*[80]

This misanthropic view of "place" is ironic, for certainly if status were a determinant of "place" as "self-acceptance" or as "self-respect", one would have assumed that Clive Morris, former "diver for pennies in the harbour", now Captain Morris, would have a place in the society. Captain Morris was taught by Franklin for whom he was a surrogate son. Rather we see an ungrateful nihilistic bitter man, a Caliban turning against his Prospero/ Franklin. Morris seems neither to accept nor love himself, nor the aunt who sacrificed for him. He does declare a love for Maria, but one can question that love, that is bred from self-hatred. His love is akin to envy. It is more like misery loving company, a misplaced notion of love.

> *I love her, I love her bad, bad, Captain. I love her like something I couldn't reach. Like something in a life that wasn't mine, the same way she felt that she couldn't share your life.*[81]

This misplaced love or rather misnamed love seems to be more a solidarity of sad souls, than a self-accepting creative encounter of self-respecting human beings. Franklin's notion of love, if love is what he feels for Maria, is clearly linked with power, possession and domination. The first inkling we have of his intentions towards her include the "abduction", a word clearly linked to force. It is tinged with illegality. He never made her his bride.

> *The bride's name is Maria. Indian girl*
> *Maria Ramsingh. You know her father, man.*
> *He's headman of Coolie Village.*
> *Widower with bags of children. Rice bags.*
> *I saw her in the fields again last week.*
> *The outcome is Clive's gone to fetch her.*
> *He's helping me with this abduction.*[82]

It is difficult to make sense of Franklin's proclamation of love, which seems indiscriminately to include animate and inanimate objects, the firmament, people and property. It is so ambiguous, on the one hand he does not "claim' these, they are given to him yet we know that he had Maria abducted", no one gave him Maria; "love is my only deed of possession" he proclaims. But what does that mean? That he loves the things he possesses or that he loves objects, people, they are his possessions? How do the stars and sea become his?

> *Those stars are mine. That sea is mine.*
> *Not because I claimed them, they were given to me.*
> *Just as you and this house and this land*
> *were given to me. By good luck, by fate.*
> *Or by love. Because I love them.*
> *Love is my only deed of possession.*[83]

This love is suspect. It does seem as though his "love" for his possessions does not last very long, he tires of them pretty quickly, as he obviously grew

161

tired of Maria. Cook, in trying to console Maria, who is drinking to appease
her loneliness while Franklin is absent on one of his frequent visits with his
English friends in Castries, says:

> . . .*you ain't know Cap'n Franklin?*
> *He does just chuck things in a corner and forget them.*
> *When he comes back from Castries you'll surprise him.*
> *But you shouldn't drink.*[84]

This attitude is the antithesis of love. People become things, objects,
play things which can be discarded once their attraction or usefulness or
both wear out. Love is not seen as shared respect, shared caring and growth
in a creative encounter. Franklin in preparing to return to England after
Maria's death, recognises his inadequacies and adds relevance to Cook's
definition of "place" as self-acceptance and self-respect, and this does not
come from one's status or possessions but in spite of them. While these may
help, they are not the answer. He says:

> . . .*I'm not a great man.*
> *It's just this property that conveyed the idea.*
> *It's a great property. Yes I am in great pain.*
> *Unutterable pain, if you'll take the hint.*[85]

Ramsingh's idea of love is to sacrifice his daughter, because he loves
himself too much. His pride will not permit him to be made a laughing stock.
He assists on her demise by providing the poison and she acquiesces in this.
Her sacrifice is understandable. The man she loves does not appreciate the gift.

Life will go on on these islands and Reverend Pritchett, the inheritor
of the mantle of Imperial mission will continue, it is hoped, to effect change
in men's lives through religion, through a Judeo-Christian God's grace, and
one hopes too that the Hindi God and the African Gods may, through
their people, dialogue towards self-respect and self-acceptance despite the
damage done by imperialism. Everyone's place will become the place where
one is most at home with oneself, a place of psychic healing and wholeness.
Cook's response to Charbon's observation that Franklin's home is England
is relevant to everyone:

> *No this is his home. The same way it is mine.*
> *The same way it is yours. Goodnight, Mr. Moses*
> *I hope you lead your people down the right road.*[86]

Walcott said in an interview years ago:

> *Think about illegitimacy in the Caribbean! Few people can claim to find their ancestry in the linear way. The whole situation in the Caribbean is an illegitimate situation. If we admit from the beginning that there is no shame in that historical bastardy then we can be men. But is we continue to sulk and say "look at what the slave-owner did", and so forth, we will never mature.*[87]

So one accepts the wound as being part of the body and claims one's place through the creative use of the wonderful diversity of culture that is one's heritage.

Yet the characters in this play seem to avoid the advantages of hybridity and syncreticity, they seem to want to pursue separate and exclusive cultural paths. They are never at home with themselves. The play's images of death and departure in a 'fading empire' seem to imply that the failure to embrace the 'Creole' ethos is a recipe for disaster. The character Jackson in Pantomime epitomises the value of the 'Creole". He is "at home" and "in his place" in a new world rich with promise and possibilities if one has the imagination to recognise it.

Conclusion

IT should be clear, from the preceding chapters, that Derek Walcott, the playwright is the embodiment of his "Creole" metaphor. He has assiduously appropriated all that he could use from the Old World and married this to the physical, cultural and psychological realities of his own New World, the Caribbean world, into which he was born and in which he assumed the Adamic role of forging a hybrid consciousness and the vocabulary of a distinct culture. He has personally validated the view of the post-colonial literary theorists concerning the importance of hybridity, syncreticity and appropriation. These, as I hope to have demonstrated above, can be seen as the cornerstone of his art. The "careful passion' that drives his art includes a formidable array of outside influences, imbibed through the playwright's formal education and continuous process of informal learning. These cultural, linguistic and genre influences came from North America, from Latin America, from Africa and from the Far East. In addition, he was fascinated by the individual New World voices of Whitman, Carpentier, Cesaire, St. John Perse, Dennis Williams, Winston Harris, Neruda, Vallejo and Paz. Their work gave him confidence and example and, together with the long familiar canonical works of Europe, entered the crucible of his imagination. What emerged was a lyrical poetry energized by a Caribbean vision and a language that has been described as pyrotechnic and masterful. But, as I have been arguing, the pressure of drama opened up language and vision even further and the plays came to embody Caribbean oral forms and a certain instantly-recognizable style or habit of being that both derives from and defines the trans-cultural reality of the Caribbean.

This is particularly well demonstrated in the adaptation of Tirso de Molina's El Burlador de Sevilla, The Joker of Seville. His use of Caribbean oral forms, the wit and risqué nature of the calypso added an exciting dimension to the old world play. The only play included in this study which does not utilize Caribbean oral forms is Walcott's youthful play Henri Christophe, where, he uses the very high-flown Jacobean style. Yet, even in his youth, Walcott's strategy is apparent. The real tragedy of Henri Christophe is that he did not appreciate his role as one of deconstructing the Imperial political culture and instead attempted to replicate that culture, the playwright uses Henri Christophe's penchant for building those castles and monuments as the metaphor for his misguided ambitions. He was structuring the wrong identification, he was privileging the hegemony of Imperial culture while ignoring the challenge implicit in the reality of the Caribbean.

This was a challenge that Walcott himself faced as a young playwright and later overcame. The playwright could see clearly that to consolidate a Eurocentric code of values in the black Caribbean could lead only to an imprisoning dead-end. Christophe turned his back on the Caribbean reality to pursue Eurocentric kingship complete with castles in the air. This was in part the fascination that this tragedy held for the young Walcott. By the time Walcott wrote O'Babylon! one of his experimental Broadway musicals, this deconstruction of the Imperial culture is achieved through the Rastafarian cult. Rude Bwoy is the successful symbol of the value of syncreticity as he arrives at stardom. He is the black star whose music is enhanced by his use of calypso, jazz and reggae, which all have value and add the infinite variety necessary for success.

It has also been part of my undertaking to demonstrate how the unique expression that is Walcott's oeuvre has proved amenable to many critical approaches. His choice of themes almost seemed to have dictated the critical approaches. His themes of Caribbean identity and the creative process are the bedrock of his 'Adamic' vision. He underscores the liberation implied in the opportunity to give things their names. It is the essence of creativity and the creative process. He questions the value of history and the claims of African triumphal nationalism as he obsessively worked and reworked these themes in his plays. I have used the post-structuralists' deconstructive approach, I have also used post-colonial theories, Womanist/feminist techniques, while noting the insights which psychology and philosophy lend to these interpretations. Jacques Derrida believed that deconstruction was a political practice, an attempt to dismantle the logic by which a particular system of thought, a political structure and social institution maintains its force. Both deconstruction and post-colonial literary theory thus have similar ends in view. What is interesting is how these theories, for obvious reasons, seem almost made to order for examining Walcott's oeuvre. A womanist/feminist technique seemed obvious for shedding light on the patriarchal discourse inherent in Joker of Seville, where women are depicted as property for disposal and objects of men's passion. The work seemed to cry out for the projection of an opposing viewpoint – especially from a woman critic. The psychology of the colonized has been extensively treated both for its pathology and for its creative possibilities. Both the Prospero/ Caliban, Robinson Crusoe characters establish paradigms for post-colonial readings of canonical works. They are seen as key figures. These figures can be mined for all the insights they give into the drama that embodies, and originates from, the encounter between coloniser and colonised.

I took the liberty to include plays under the following headings: Folk Plays, Historical Plays, Experimental Broadway Musical Plays and Psychological Plays. The folk plays seemed to create the pristine atmosphere of a Garden of Eden where man is just beginning to comprehend the magnitude of the responsibility of personhood. Walcott himself felt the need to write about unaccommodated man. In Ti-Jean the devil wishes to experience human emotions. Malcochon examines the themes of responsibility, sin, salvation, the dilemma of free choice which man faces. Here was the challenge of the Adamic vision, by using the folk play idiom he was able to construct plays in the folk play tradition while using Caribbean language and ordinary Caribbean characters. He was on his way to explore the theory of "creolization".

In Dream on Monkey Mountain, the question of identity is directly addressed as Makak is asked the question, what is your name? Who is he? What should he be called? The playwright explores this Caribbean dilemma by way of myth within Caribbean culture. It is also through the natural scenery of sea and forest that those myths materialize.

In the chapter on Historical Plays, both Henri Christophe and The Last Carnival are securely grounded in history. Haiti, the first independent black republic in the New World exists because of European colonization and slavery. The rhetoric of the French Revolution and the theories of republicanism played a part. Henri Christophe is a historical figure. He is one of the former slaves who lead the revolt against their former masters. The Last Carnival depicts elements of Trinidad history, that is the arrival of the French in Trinidad via Guadeloupe, Martinique and Grenada. These new arrivals were mainly plantation owners who came with their slaves. They were brought into Trinidad to solve the problem of white management, since the Spaniards seemed inadequate to the task. In both plays then, the confrontation between French culture and African labour becomes not only a fruitful topos for Walcott's dramatic invention, but also part of the rich cultural hybridity encoded in the lives, visions and understandings of all West Indians – almost as though these were encoded genetically. In Henri Christophe, Walcott and the reader/audience encounter a version of Caribbean man, as irredeemably Creole as we all are. Whereas Henri Christophe's total identification with French culture destroys him, the la Fontaine heirs are consciously "Creole" and identify with the reality of "place" that is Trinidad. The art which this syncreticity produces becomes the metaphor of the creative process, appropriation, abrogation, hybridity and syncreticity triumph – the creativity of carnival – over the isolationist stance of the efforts of the Black power advocates. Thus the strategy employed in Henri Christophe is itself a cautionary tale which the playwright underscores by using the Jacobean style of writing which totally identifies with the hegemony of the Imperial canons while ignoring the wealth inherent in the culture of the Caribbean. The Last Carnival interrogates Imperial culture. It is counter-discursive, as it relocates the cultural centre in the Caribbean.

The experimental Broadway musical plays O'Babylon! and The Joker of Seville provide Walcott the opportunity to incorporate the musical expressions of the Caribbean. While there is a clear understanding by the playwright that Caribbean musical forms must be an integral part of his drama, he expresses his delight at the ease with which Tirso's play could be appropriated. The Creole metaphor is emphasised by him in the Trinidad setting. Its Spanish past, the risqué, racy calypso, the dance all come together in creating a package for a musical. It is the assumptions of the patriarchal discourse in The Joker of Seville which not only invite a womanist/feminist interpretation but question the negative assumptions of the Freudians about women. These notions lead to the 'women-enjoyed-being-raped' heresy of Don Juan's exploits. O'Babylon! seems to be a musical jazzed up version of Dream as Walcott assiduously works and reworks, through the Rastafarians, the post-colonial themes of place, appropriation, abrogation. The Rastafarians deconstruct the Imperial discourse, in the subversive use of language, in their syncretic religion and in their social institutions, while affirming their rootedness in the African experience. Here Rude Bwoy is the symbol of this syncreticity. He uses the medium of music to become a Black star as he appropriates reggae, jazz and calypso on his way to stardom.

The chapter which I deemed psychological contains Remembrance, Pantomime and Franklin. They are all discourses on the Imperialist adventure and its consequences in terms of human behaviour. Of course, this is the stuff of which post-colonial literature is formed. This fateful encounter between coloniser and colonised has been treated creatively by Shakespeare in The Tempest and it has been examined by psychologists and sociologists. The key literary figures are Prospero and Caliban. Walcott's fascination with the castaway figure of Robinson Crusoe arises from seeing him as emblematic of the possibilities inherent in structuring a life out of nothing, of beginning anew, as the playwright himself had to do with respect to his art. There is clearly a pattern, therefore, where the characters and situations in the play echo important aspects of the real situation of the playwright, and of course of the playwright as representative of West Indian people. In a very real sense, therefore, Walcott is writing himself: dramatizing the conflicts in his own blood, inventing and objectifying the Creole person and his world as a mirror in which we can all see who we are. This no doubt helps explain why his art is "a careful passion".

In this way, therefore, Jackson and Henry Trewe of Pantomime, Perez Jordan of Remembrance and Franklin and his household in Franklin are all what George Lamming would call "natives of our person"; they belong to us not in the traditional way of memorable literary characters, but in a defining or identifying sense. They are not just interesting, but important and instructive, in terms of the social and cultural reality we are attempting to forge in the Caribbean.

End Notes

INTRODUCTION

1   Edward Kamau Brathwaite, *Barabajan Poems* (Kingston & New York: Savacou North, 1994) 90.

2   Derek Walcott, *"What the Twilight Says: An Overture,"* Dream on Monkey Mountain and Other Plays (London: Jonathan Cape,1972) 36.

3   Derek Walcott, *"Outlook for a National Theatre,"* Sunday Guardian, November 6, 1974.

4   Walcott, *"What the Twilight Says: An Overture,"* 6.

CHAPTER ONE

1   Walcott, *"What the Twilight Says,"* 23-4.

2   Laurence A. Breiner, *"Walcott's Early Drama,"* The Art of Derek Walcott, ed. Steward Brown. (Glamorgan: Poetry Wales Press Ltd , 1991) 78-9.

3   Philip Wheelwright, *"Poetry, Myth and Reality,"* The Language of Poetry, ed. Allen Tate (New York: Russell and Russell, 1960) 6-7.

4   Breiner, "Walcott's Early Drama," 77.

5   Robert D. Hammer, *Derek Walcott* (Boston: Twayne Publishers, 1981) 69.

6   Derek Walcott, *Dream on Monkey Mountain and Other Plays* (London: Jonathan Cape Ltd, 1972) 108.

7   *Ibid.,* 115.

8   *Ibid.,* 115.

9   *Ibid.,* 116.

10   *Ibid.,* 116.

11   *Ibid.,* 116.

12   *Ibid.,* 117.

13   *Ibid.,* 135.

14   *Ibid.,* 136.

15   *Ibid.,* 137.

16   *Ibid.,* 137.

17   *Ibid.,* 137-8.

18   *Ibid.,* 162.

19   *Ibid.,* 162.

20   *Ibid.,* 166.

21   *Ibid.,* 95.

22   *Ibid.,* 103.

23   *Ibid.*, 133.
24   *Ibid.*, 133-4.
25   *Ibid.*, 108.
26   *Ibid.*, 117.
27   *Ibid.*, 121.
28   *Ibid.*, 129-30.
29   *Ibid.*, 131.
30   *Ibid.*, 143.
31   *Ibid.*, 157.
32   *Ibid.*, 157.
33   *Ibid.*, 163.
34   Michel Foucault, *"What is An Author?" Textual Strategies. Perspectives on Post-Structuralist Criticism*, ed. Tusé V. Harare (New York: Cornell University Press, 1979) 158.
35   Foucault, *"What is an Author?"* 158.
36   Breiner, *"Walcott's Early Drama,"* 78.
37   Culler, *On Deconstruction*, 86.
38   Walcott, *Dream*, 326.
39   *Ibid.*, 216.
40   *Ibid.*, 228.
41   *Ibid.*, 214.
42   *Ibid.*, 229.
43   *Ibid.*, 304.
44   *Ibid.*, 235.
45   *Ibid.*, 256.
46   *Ibid.*, 221-2.
47   *Ibid.*, 223.
48   *Ibid.*, 326.
49   *Ibid.*, 325.
50   *Ibid.*, 251.
51   *Ibid.*, 253.
52   *Ibid.*, 267.
53   *Ibid.*, 248.
54   *Ibid.*, 291.
55   *Ibid.*, 289.
56   *Ibid.*, 292-3.
57   *Ibid.*, 303.
58   *Ibid.*, 301.
59   *Ibid.*, 283.
60   *Ibid.*, 315.
61   *Ibid.*, 310.
62   *Ibid.*, 319.
63   Said, *The World, the Text and the Critic*, 203.
64   *Ibid.*,184.
65   *Ibid.*, 184.
66   Hamner, *Derek Walcott*, 73-4.
67   *Ibid.* 178.
68   *Ibid.* 197.
69   *Ibid.* 195.
70   *Ibid.* 202.
71   *Ibid.* 181.

72   *Ibid.* 182.
73   *Ibid.* 182.
74   *Ibid.* 174.
75   *Ibid.* 188.
76   *Ibid.* 199.
77   *Ibid.* 199.
78   *Ibid.* 196.
79   *Ibid.* 199-200.
80   *Ibid.* 200.
81   *Ibid.* 198.
82   *Ibid.* 176.
83   *Ibid.* 193.
84   *Ibid.* 202.
85   Said, *The World, the Text and the Critic,* 185.

CHAPTER TWO

1   Bill Ashcroft, Gareth Griffiths and Helen Tiffin, *The Empire Writes Back. Theory and Practice in Post-Colonial Literatures* (London: Routledge, 1989) 2.
2   Ashcroft, Griffiths and Tiffin, *Ibid.* 7.
3   *Ibid.* 169.
4   Edward Said, *Culture and Imperialism* (New York: Alfred A. Knopf Inc, 1993) 252-3.
5   James Anthony Froude, *The English in the West Indies OR the Bow of Ulysees* (London: Longmans, Green and Co. 1882) 302.
6   *Ibid.* 306.
7   Said, *Culture and Imperialism,* 246.
8   *Ibid.* 253.
9   Derek Walcott, *Henri Christophe* (Barbados Advocate Co. 1950) 5.
10   *Ibid.* 5.
11   Said, *Culture and Imperialism,* Introduction xii.
12   Derek Walcott, *The Last Carnival* (New York: Farrar, Straus and Giroux, 1986) 19.
13   *Ibid.* 42.
14   *Ibid.* 73.
15   *Ibid.* 84.
16   Walcott, *Henri Christophe,* 56.
17   Said, *Culture and Imperialism,* 336.
18   *Ibid.* 259.
19   *Ibid.* 258.
20   Walcott, *Henri Christophe,* 10.
21   *Ibid.*7.
22   *Ibid.*50.
23   *Ibid.*40.
24   *Ibid.*40.
25   *Ibid.*40-1.
26   *Ibid.*41.
27   *Ibid.*51.
28   *Ibid.*51.
29   Froude, *The English in the West Indies,* 304.
30   *Ibid.*7.

31   Walcott, *Henri Christophe*, 4.

32   *Ibid*.4.

33   *Ibid*.4.

34   *Ibid*.5.

35   *Ibid*.18.

36   *Ibid*.23.

37   *Ibid*.24.

38   *Ibid*.23.

39   *Ibid*.23.

40   Ashcroft, Griffiths and Tiffin, *The Empire Writes Back*, 33.

41   Walcott, *Henri Christophe*, I.

42   *Ibid*.11.

43   *Ibid*.12.

44   *Ibid*.12.

45   *Ibid*.17.

46   *Ibid*.36.

47   *Ibid*.36.

48   *Ibid*.59.

49   J. J. Thomas, Froudacity – *West Indian Fables by James Anthony Froude Explained* by J. J. Thomas, author of the Creole Grammar (London, 2 Albert Road: New Beacon Books Ltd., 1889)93.

50   Ashcroft, Griffiths and Tiffin, *The Empire Writes Back*, 167-8.

51   Edward Hirsch, Interview with Derek Walcott in St. Lucia, 15 June 1985.

52   Ashcroft, Griffith and Tiffin, *The Empire Writes Back*, 170-4.

53   Said, *Culture and Imperialism*, 314.

54   Derek Walcott, *Another Life* (London. Jonathan Cape, 1973) 77.

55   Eric Williams, *History of the People of Trinidad and Tobago* (London: Andre Deutsch Ltd., 1964) 40.

56   Walcott, *History of the People*, 47-8

57   Derek Walcott, "*The Last Carnival*," *Three Plays* (New York: Farrar, Straus and Giroux, 1968) 56.

58   Kim Johnson, "*Trinidad Carnival*," Caribbean Quarterly.

59   Hamner, *Derek Walcott*, 94-5.

60   Said, *Culture and Imperialism*, 259.

61   Ashcroft, Griffiths and Tiffin, *The Empire Writes Back*, 28.

62   Walcott, *The Muse of History*, 4.

63   *Ibid*. 2-3.

64   Walcott, *The Last Carnival*, 6.

65   *Ibid*. 19.

66   *Ibid*. 17.

67   *Ibid*. 39.

68   Ashcroft, Griffiths and Tiffin, *The Empire Writes Back*, 44.

69   Walcott, *The Last Carnival*, 44-5.

70   *Ibid*. 46.

71   *Ibid*. 50.

72   *Ibid*. 76.

73   *Ibid*. 31.

74   *Ibid*. 76.

75   *Ibid*. 54.

76   *Ibid*. 59.

77   *Ibid.* 59.

78   Hirsch, Interview.

79   Eric Williams, Nation Newspaper, Trinidad, June 26, 1964.

80   Selwyn D. Ryan, *Race and Nationalism in Trinidad and Tobago, A study of Decolonization in a Multi-Racial Society* (Toronto: Toronto U P, 1972) 456.

81   C. L. R. James, *Spheres of Existence. Selected Writings* (London: Allison and Busby Ltd., 1980) 180.

82   Walcott, *The Last Carnival*, 78.

83   *Ibid.* 89.

84   *Ibid.* 92-3.

85   *Ibid.* 99-100.

CHAPTER THREE

1   Derek Walcott, *The Joker of Seville and O'Babylon!* (New York: Farrar, Straus and Giroux, 1978) 269.

2   Homi K. Bhabha, *Nation and Narration* (New York: Routledge, 1990) 296.

3   Walcott, *The Joker of Seville*, 224.

4   Thomas, *Froudacity*, 51.

5   Said, *Culture and Imperialism*, 228-9.

6   Hirsch Interview, St. Lucia 1986.

7   Edward Brathwaite, *Rights of Passage* (London: Oxford U P, 1967)77.

8   Walcott, *The Joker of Seville*, 167.

9   Tony Martin, *Marcus Garvey, Hero: A First Biography* (Massachusetts: The Majority Press, 1983) 55.

10   Frantz Fanon, *The Wretched of the Earth*, 1963.

11   Walcott, *The Joker of Seville*, 164.

12   *Ibid.* 161.

13   Bhabha, *Nation and Narration*, 296.

14   Walcott, *The Joker of Seville*, 176.

15   *Ibid.* 177.

16   *Ibid.* 181.

17   *Ibid.* 265.

18   *Ibid.* 272.

19   *Ibid.* 172.

20   *Ibid.* 209.

21   *Ibid.* 195.

22   *Ibid.* 217.

23   *Ibid.* 263.

24   *Ibid.* 220.

25   *Ibid.* 254.

26   Hamner, *Derek Walcott*, 121.

27   Walcott, *The Joker of Seville*, 222.

28   *Ibid.* 269.

29   Said, *Culture and Imperialism*, 332.

30   See Henry Louis Gates, Jr. ed., *Reading Black Reading Feminist: A Critical Anthology* (New York: Penguin Books Inc., 1990).

31   See Carole Boyce Davies and Elaine Savory Fido eds. *Out of the Kumbla: Caribbean Women and Literature* (New Jersey: Africa World Press Inc., 1990).

32   See *Sigmund Freud, the Volumes in the Pelican Freud Library Introductory Lectures on Psycho-analysis. The Interpretation of Dreams: on Sexuality and the Case Histories* (London: Harmondsworth, 1973).

33   See Luce Irigaray, Carolyn G. Heilburn and Nancy K. Miller eds., *An Ethics of Sexual Difference* (N. Y. Ithaca: Cornell University Press, 1993).

34   *Ibid.*

35   *Ibid.*

36   Walcott, *The Joker of Seville*, 141-142.

37   Derek Walcott, Trinidad Guardian. Nov. 6, 1974.

38   Walcott, *The Joker of Seville*, 112.

39   Lemuel A. Johnson, *"Abeng: (Re)Calling the body in (To) Question" Out of the Kumbla*, eds. Carole Boyce Davies and Elaine Savory Fido (New Jersey: Africa World Press, 1990) 111-142.

40   Walcott, *The Joker of Seville*, 131.

41   Johnson, *"Abeng,"* 127.

42   Walcott, *The Joker of Seville*, 81.

43   *Ibid.* 28.

44   *Ibid.* 29.

45   *Ibid.* 36.

46   *Ibid.* 114.

47   Hamner, *Derek Walcott*, 111.

48   Walcott, *The Joker of Seville*, 138.

49   *Ibid.* 19.

50   *Ibid.* 31.

51   *Ibid.* 37.

52   *Ibid.* 109.

53   *Ibid.* 14.

54   Johnson, *"Abeng,"* 127-128.

55   Walcott, *The Joker of Seville*, 48.

56   *Ibid.* 144-145.

57   *Ibid.* 117.

58   *Ibid.* 8.

59   *Ibid.* 10.

60   Elaine Scarry, *"The Body in Pain. The Making and Unmaking of the World," Out of the Kumbla*, eds. Carole Boyce Davies and Elaine Savory Fido (New Jersey: Africa World Press Inc., 1990)

61   Johnson, *"Abeng,"* 127-128.

62   Walcott, *The Joker of Seville*, 40.

63   *Ibid.* 40.

64   *Ibid.* 43.

65   *Ibid.* 43.

66   *Ibid.* 47.

67   *Ibid.* 68.

68   *Ibid.* 76.

69   *Ibid.* 95.

70   *Ibid.* 104.

71   *Ibid.* 109.

72   *Ibid.* 112.

73   *Ibid.* 118.

74   *Ibid.* 149.

75   Johnson, *"Abeng,"* 129-130.

CHAPTER FOUR

I   Said, *Culture and Imperialism*, 212.
2   Ashcroft, Griffiths and Tiffin, *The Empire Writes Back*, 190.
3   O. Mannoni, *Prospero and Caliban The Psychology of Colonization* (New York: Praeger. Inc., 1964) 17.
4   Frantz Fanon, *Black Skins White Masks* (New York: Grove Press Inc., 1967) 8.
5   George Lamming, *Pleasures of Exile* (London: Michael Joseph, 1960) 107.
6   Wynter, *"Beyond Miranda's Meanings"* 355-366.
7   Said, *Culture and Imperialism*, 212.
8   Ashcroft, Griffiths and Tiffin, *The Empire Writes Back*, 9.
9   Wynter, *"Beyond Miranda's Meanings,"* 356.
10 Ashcroft, Griffiths and Tiffin, *The Empire Writes Back*, 12.
11 Said, *Culture and Imperialism*, 213.
12 Ashcroft, Griffiths and Tiffin, *The Empire Writes Back*, 44.
13 Derek Walcott, *Remembrance and Pantomime* (New York: Farrar, Strauss and Giroux, 1980) 7.
14 *Ibid.* 8.
15 *Ibid.* 9.
16 *Ibid.* 9.
17 William Shakespeare, *The Tempest*, Act III.II, II.98-103, The Riverside Shakespeare (Boston: Houghton Mifflin Company, 1974) 1626
18 Shakespeare, *The Tempest*, Act I.II, II. 335-336.
19 *Ibid.* 148-152.
20 *Ibid.* 184-187.
21 Walcott, *Remembrance and Pantomime*, 13.
22 *Ibid.* 27.
23 *Ibid.* 28.
24 *Ibid.* 27.
25 *Ibid.* 28.
26 *Ibid.* 29.
27 Said, *Culture and Imperialism*, 212.
28 Walcott, *Remembrance and Pantomime*, 31.
29 *Ibid.* 32.
30 Wynter, *"Beyond Miranda's Meanings,"* 360.
31 *Ibid.* 11.
32 *Ibid.* 33.
33 *Ibid.* 25.
34 *Ibid.* 34.
35 *Ibid.* 38-39.
36 *Ibid.* 40.
37 *Ibid.* 44.
38 *Ibid.* 44.
39 *Ibid.* 56.
40 *Ibid.* 72.
41 *Ibid.* 73.
42 *Ibid.* 73.
43 Shakespeare, *The Tempest*, Act III.II, II. 100-103.

44   Walcott, *Remembrance and Pantomime*, 86.

45   Ashcroft, Griffiths and Tiffin, *The Empire Writes Back*, 170-171.

46   *Ibid.* 52.

47   Walcott, *Remembrance and Pantomime*, 148.

48   Said, *Culture and Imperialism*, 296.

49   Mannoni, *Prospero and Caliban*, 103.

50   Walcott, *Remembrance and Pantomime*, 95-96.

51   *Ibid.* 112-113.

52   *Ibid.* 114.

53   Ashcroft, Griffiths and Tiffin, *The Empire Writes Back*, 77.

54   Froude, *The English in the West Indies*, 87.

55   Thomas, *Froudacity*, 190.

56   Walcott, *Remembrance and Pantomime*, 125.

57   *Ibid.* 126.

58   Mannoni, *Prospero and Caliban*, 100.

59   Walcott, *Remembrance and Pantomime*, 155.

60   *Ibid.* 169.

61   Ashcroft, Griffiths and Tiffin, *The Empire Writes Back*, 8-9.

62   Derek Walcott, Franklin, *A Tale of the Islands* (New York: Unpublished, Author's Agent Bridget Aschenberg ICM, 1989) 55.

63   *Ibid.* 48.

64   *Ibid.* 4.

65   *Ibid.* 57.

66   *Ibid.* 51.

67   *Ibid.* 66.

68   *Ibid.* 24.

69   *Ibid.* 27.

70   *Ibid.* 27.

71   *Ibid.* 28.

72   *Ibid.* 49.

73   *Ibid.* 52.

74   Ashcroft, Griffiths and Tiffin, *The Empire Writes Back*, 172.

75   Walcott, *Franklin*, 44.

76   *Ibid.* 43.

77   *Ibid.* 47.

78   *Ibid.* 50.

79   *Ibid.* 53.

80   *Ibid.* 63.

81   *Ibid.* 72.

82   *Ibid.* 9.

83   *Ibid.* 18.

84   *Ibid.* 22.

85   *Ibid.* 67.

86   *Ibid.* 7.

87   Derek Walcott, Interview: *The Art of Poetry.*

Bibliography

PRIMARY SOURCES, A

WALCOTT, Derek. *Dream on Monkey Mountain and Other Plays*. London: Jonathan Cape, 1972.

---. *"Drums and Colours."* Caribbean Quarterly 7.1-2 (1961) 1-104.

---. *"Franklin: A Tale of the Islands"*. Unpublished, c. 1961.

---. *"Harry Dernier, A Play for Radio Production."* Bridgetown: Barbados Advocate, 1952.

---. *Henri Christophe. A Chronicle in Seven Scenes.* Bridgetown, Barbados: Advocate Co., 1950.

---. *"In a Fine Castle."* Unpublished, 1970.

---. *Ione.* Mona, Jamaica: Extra-Mural Department, 1957.

---. *The Joker of Seville and O'Babylon!* London: Jonathan Cape, 1979.

---. *"The Joker of Seville to be staged Gayelle-Style."* Sunday Guardian 17 November 1974:7.

---. *"Jourmard."* Unpublished, 1967.

---. *"Marie La Veau."* Trinidad and Tobago Review Literary Supplement 3-6.

---. *"The Matadors."* Unpublished, 1974.

---. *Omeros.* New York: Farrar, Straus and Giroux, 1990.

---. *Remembrance and Pantomime.* New York: Farrar, Straus and Giroux, 1980.

---. *Three Plays: The Last Carnival, Beef no Chicken, A Branch of the Blue Nile.* New York: Farrar, Straus and Giroux, 1986.

PRIMARY SOURCES, B

"Carnival Spirit a Contempt for Material Treasures." Sunday Guardian 24 February

1963: 10.

"Carnival: The Theatre of the Streets." Sunday Guardian 9 February 1964: 4.

"Derek Walcott looks at Off-Broadway Theatre." Sunday Guardian 20 October 1963: 15.

"Derek Walcott talks about The Joker of Seville." Carib 4 (1986): 1-15.

"The Figure of Crusoe; on the Theme of Isolation in West Indian Writing." Open Lecture Series, University of the West Indies, 27 October 1965.

"Good Times, Wonderful Times: The Travels and Joys of a Touring Company." Unpublished, 1971.

"The Joker: Closer to Continuous Theatre." Trinidad Guardian 22 March 1975: 5.

"The Little Carib Theatre Workshop," Opus 1.1 (1960): 31.

"Meanings," Savacou 2 (1970): 45-51.

"The Muse of History: An Essay." Is Massa Day Dead? Black Moods in the Caribbean. Ed. Orde Coombs. New York: Doubleday, 1974. 1-28.

"Outlook for a National theatre." Sunday Guardian 6 November 1974: 4.

"Theatre and the Tents in Trinidad." Tapia 7.2 (1977): 6-7.

Introduction *"What the Twilight Says: An Overture."* Dream on Monkey Mountain and Other Plays by Walcott. New York: Farrar, Straus and Giroux, 1970: 3-40.

"Why This Astigmatism Towards the Workshop's White Actors?" Trinidad Guardian 19 April 1973: 5.

SECONDARY SOURCES

ALLEN, Walter. *The English Novel: A Short Critical History.* Harmondsworth, Mx: Penguin Books Ltd., 1954.

ANGELOU, Maya. *Oh Pray My Wings are Gonna Fit Me Well.* New York: Random House, 1975.

ASHCROFT, Bill, Gareth Griffiths and Helen Tiffin. *The Empire Writes Back. Theory and Practice in Post-Colonial Literatures.* New York: Routledge, 1989.

AUGUSTUS, Earl. *"In a Fine Castle."* Trinidad Express 7 November 1971: 17+.

BACON, Francis. *The Advancement of Learning.* London: J. M. Dent & Sons, 1962.

BAKHTIN, Mikhail Mikhailovich. *The Dialogic Imagination.* Austin: U of Texas P, 1981.

BAPTISTE, Owen. *"The Music of the Caribbean,"* People April 1976: 5.

BARTHES, Roland. *Image Music Text.* New York: Hill & Wang, 1977.

---. *"From Work to Text."* *Textual Strategies Perspectives in Post-Structualist Criticism.* Ed. Josué V. Harari. Ithaca: Cornell UP, 1979.

BAUGH, Edward. *Derek Walcott: Memory as Vision: Another Life.* London: Longman Group Ltd., 1978.

---. *"The West Indian Writer and His Quarrel with History."* Tapia 20 February 1977: 6-7.

BECKLES, Hilary. *History of Barbados.* Cambridge: Cambridge UP, 1990.

---. *Natural Rebels: A Social History of Enslaved Black Women in Barbados.* London: Zed Books Ltd., 1989.

BERNAL, Martin. *Black Athena: The Afroasiatic Roots of Classical Civilization.* New Jersey: Rutgers UP, 1987.

BHABHA, Homi K., ed. *Nation and Narration.* New York: Routledge, 1990.

BRATHWAITE, Edward. *Rights of Passage.* London: Oxford UP, 1967.

---. *Islands.* London: Oxford UP, 1969.

---. *Masks.* London: Oxford UP, 1968.

---. *Other Exiles.* London: Oxford UP, 1975.

---. *Zea Mexican Diaries.* Madison: U of Wisconsin P, 1993.

BRECHT, Bertolt. *The Caucasian Chalk Circle.* Trans. James Stern and Tama Stern. London: Methuen, 1984.

BREINER, Lawrence. *"Lyric and Autobiography in West Literature."* Journal of West Indian Literature 3.1 (1983): 3-15.

---. *"Walcott's Early Drama."* *The Art of Derek Walcott.* Ed. Stewart Brown, Bridgend, Mid Glamorgan: Seren Books, 1991.

BRERETON, Bridget. *Race Relations in Colonial Trinidad 1870 – 1900.* Cambridge: Cambridge UP, 1979.

BRODBER, Erna. *Jane and Louisa Will Soon Come Home.* London: New Beacon Books, 1980.

---. *Perceptions of Caribbean Women: Towards a Documentation of Stereotypes.* Cave Hill, Barbados: Institute of Social and Economic Research, 1982.

BRODSKY, Joseph. *Less Than One.* Harmondsworth, Mx: Penguin Books, 1987.

BROWN, Stewart. *The Art of Derek Walcott*. Bridgend, Mid Glamorgan: Seren Books, 1991.

BURKE, Paul. *C. L. R. James: The Artist as Revolutionary*. London: Verso, 1980.

CARNEGIE, Jeniphier R. *Critics on West Indian Literature. A Selected Bibliography*. Mona, Jamaica: Research and Publications Committee, 1979.

CESAIRE, Aime. *Cahier d'un Retour Au Pays Natal*. Paris: Presence Africaine, 1979.

CHINWEIZU. *Decolonizing the African Mind*. Lagos: Peru Press, 1987.

CHINWEIZU, Jemie Onwuchekwa and Madubuike Ihechukwu. *Towards the Decolonization of African Literature*. Washington: Howard UP, 1983.

CICCARELLI, Sharon L. *"Reflections Before and After Carnival: An Interview with Derek Walcott." Chant of Saints: A Gathering of Afro-American Literature, Art and Scholarship*. Eds. Michael S. Harper and Robert B. Hamner. Urbana: U of Illinois P, 1979. 296-309.

CIXOUS, Hélène. *"The Laugh of the Medusa."* Signs: Journal of Women in Culture and Society 1-4 (1976): 875-93.

CLIFF, Michelle. *Abeng*. New York: The Crossing Press, 1984.

COOMBS, Orde. *Is Massa day Dead? Black Moods in the Caribbean.* New York: Doubleday, 1974.

CULLER, Jonathan. *On Deconstruction: Theory and Criticism After Structuralism*. Ithaca: Cornell UP, 1982.

CURTIN, Philip. *Two Jamaicas, the Role of Ideas in a Tropical Colony (1830-1865)*. Cambridge: Howard UP, 1955.

DAVIES, Carole Boyce & Elaine Savory-Fido, eds. *Out of the Kumbla. Caribbean Women in Literature*. Lawrenceville, NJ: Africa World Press Inc., 1990.

"Death of our Dodos in The Last Carnival: A play of Rare Quality. Camps in an Unlovely Tent." Trinidad Guardian 15 July 1982: 18.

DERRIDA, Jacques. *Margins of Philosophy*. Chicago: U of Chicago P, 1982.

DE VERTEUIL, Anthony. *Sir Louis de Verteuil His Life and Times*. Port-of-Spain, Trinidad: Columbus Publishers Ltd., 1973.

EAGLETON, Terry. *Literary Theory: An Introduction*. Oxford: Basil Blackwell, 1983.

EVANS, Mari. *Black Women Writers (1950-1980)*. New York: Anchor Books, 1984.

EYSENCK, H. J. *Uses and Abuses of Psychology.* Harmondsworth, Mx: Penguin Books Ltd., 1953.

FANON, Frantz. *Black Skin White Masks.* New York: Grove Press, 1967.

---. *A Dying Colonialism.* New York: Grove Press, 1965.

---. *The Wretched of the Earth.* New York: Wheatland Corporation, 1963.

FERGUSON, James. *Papa Doc, Baby Doc, Haiti and the Duvaliers.* Oxford: Basil Blackwell Ltd., 1987.

FIDO, Elaine. *"Walcott and Sexual Politics: Macho Conventions Shape the Moon."* The Literary Half-Yearly 26.1 (1985): 43-60.

FISH, Stanley. *Is There a Text in this Class?* Cambridge: Harvard UP, 1980.

FOUCAULT, Michel. *A Critical Reader.* Oxford: Basil Blackwell Ltd., 1986.

---. *"What is an Author?" Textual Strategies. Perspectives in Post-Structuralist Criticism.* Ed. Tusé Harare. New York: Cornell U P, 1979. 141-160.

---. *The Order of Things: An Archaeology of the Human Sciences.* New York: Vintage Books, 1973.

FRASER, G. S. *The Modern Writer and His World.* London: Andre Deutsch, 1964.

FREUD, Sigmund. *The Interpretation of Dreams.* New York: Basic Books, 1955.

FROUDE, James Anthony. *The English in the West Indies or the Bow of Ulysees.* London: Longmans, Green and Co., 1888.

GARVEY, Amy Jacques, ed. *The Philosophy and Opinions of Marcus Garvey or Africa for the Africans.* London: The Majority Press, 1986.

GATES, Henry Louis. *Black Literature and Literary Theory.* New York: Methuen Inc., 1984.

---. *The Signifying Monkey: A Theory of Afro-American Literary Criticism.* Oxford: Oxford UP, 1988.

---. *Figures in Black, Words, Signs and the 'Racial' Self.* Oxford: Oxford UP, 1989.

---. Ed. *Reading Black, Reading Feminist: A Critical Anthology.* Harmondsworth, Mx: Penguin Books, 1990.

GILMORE, Myron P. *The World of Humanism.* New York: Harper & Row Inc., 1962.

GRAVES, Robert. *The Greek Myths.* Harmondsworth, Mx: Peguin Books Ltd., 1955.

HAMNER, Robert D. *Derek Walcott.* Boston: Twayne Publishers, 1981.

---. *Critical Perspectives on Derek Walcott.* Washington: Three Continents Press, 1993.

HARARI, Josue V. Ed. *Textual Strategies: Perspectives in Post Structuralist Criticism.* Ithaca, New York: Cornell UP, 1979.

HARRIS, Wilson. *Carnival.* London: Faber and Faber Ltd., 1985.

HILL, Errol. *Plays for Today.* Harlow: Longman Group Ltd., 1985.

---. *The Trinidad Carnival: Mandate for a National Theatre.* Austin: U of Texas P, 1972.

HIRSCH, E. D. *The Aims of Interpretation.* Chicago: Chicago UP, 1976.

HIRSCH, Edward. *"The Art of Poetry. XXXVII Interview with Derek Walcott in St. Lucia."* Paris Review 101 (1986): 197-230.

HUXLEY, Aldous. *The Perennial Philosophy.* London: Chatto & Windus, 1946.

IRIGARAY, Luce. *An Ethics of Sexual Difference.* Trans. Carolyn Burke and Gillian C. Gill. New York: Cornell UP Ltd., 1993.

ISMOND, Patricia. *"Breaking Myths and Maidenheads."* Review of The Joker of Seville by Derek Walcott. Tapia 18 May 1975: 4+

---. *"Breaking Myths and Maidenheads."* Review of Joker of Seville by Derek Walcott. Tapia 1 June 1975: 6-8.

---. *"Walcott's Later Drama: From Joker to Remembrance."* Ariel 16.3 (1985): 89-101.

JAMES, C. L. R. *The Artist in the Caribbean.* Mona: University College of the West Indies, 1970.

---. *Spheres of "Existence". Selected Writings.* London: Allison and Busby Ltd., 1980.

Black Jacobins. New York: Vintage Books, 1989.

JOHNSON, Barbara. *The Critical Difference: Essays in the Contemporary Rhetoric of Reading.* Baltimore: John Hopkins UP, 1980.

JOHNSON, Kim. *"Trinidad Carnival."* Caribbean Quarterly 18 (1972): 86-101.

JOHNSON, Lemuel. *"Abeng (Re)Calling the Body in (to) Question."* Out of the Kumbla. Caribbean Women Writers in Literature. Eds. Carol Boyce Davies and Elaine Savory Fido. Lawrenceville, NJ: Africa World Press Inc., 1990. 111-142.

KANT, Immanuel. *Critique of Practical Reason and Other Works on the Theory of Ethics.* London: Longman, Green and Co. Ltd., 1909.

KRISTEVA, Julia. *La Révolution du Langage Poétique*. Paris: Edition de Seuil, 1974.

LAMONT, Corliss. *The Philosophy of Humanism*. London: Barrie & Rockliff, 1965.

LIVERPOOL, Hollis. *'Carnival in Trinidad and Tobago.'* Diss. U of the West Indies, 1977.

LOGAN, Rayford W. *Haiti and the Dominican Republic*. Oxford: Oxford UP, 1968.

LOVELACE, Earl. *Review of The Last Carnival by Derek Walcott*. Trinidad Express 25 July 1982: 15+.

MANNONI, O. *Prospero and Caliban the Phychology of Colonization*. New York: Frederick A. Praeger Inc., 1964.

MARTIN, Tony. *Marcus Garvey Hero. A First Biography*. Dover, Massachussets: The Majority Press, 1983.

MBITI, John S. *African Religious and Philosophy*. London: Heinemann Educational Books Ltd., 1969.

MILLER, Nancy K. *The Poetics of Gender: Gender and Culture*. New York: Columbia UP, 1986.

NETTLEFORD, Rex M. *Mirror, Mirror, Identity, Race and Protest in Jamaica*. London: Collins Clear Type Press, 1970.

PEYRE, Henri. *The Failures of Criticism*. Ithaca: Cornell UP, 1967.

ROBERTS, Peter A. *West Indians and Their Language*. Cambridge: Cambridge UP, 1988.

ROHLEHR, Gordon. *The Shape of That Hurt and Other Essays*. Port-of-Spain, Trinidad: Longman Trinidad Ltd., 1992.

---. *"History as Absurdity." Is Massa Day Dead? Black Moods in the Caribbean*. Ed. Orde Coombs. New York: Doubleday, 1974. 69-110.

---. *"The Three Stages of Black Revolution: A Brief Look at Derek Walcott's Ti-Jean and His Brothers."* Liberation September 1970.

RYAN, Selwyn D. *Race and Nationalism in Trinidad and Tobago: A Study of Decolonization in a Multi-racial Society*. Toronto: U of Toronto P, 1972.

---. *Trinidad and Tobago. The Independence Experience 1962-1987*. St. Augustine, Trinidad: institute of Social and Economic Research, 1988.

SAAKANA, Amon Saba. *The Colonial Legacy in Caribbean Literature*. London:

Karnak House, 1987.

SAID, Edward W. *Orientalism*. London: Routledge and Kegan Paul Ltd., 1978.

---. *The World, the Text and the Critic*. Cambridge: Harvard UP, 1983.

---. *Culture and Imperialism*. New York: Alfred A. Knopf Inc., 1983.

SCARRY, Elaine. *"The Body in Pain; the Making and Un/making of the World."* Out of the Kumbla. Caribbean Women Writers in Literature. Eds. Carole Boyce Davies and Elaine Savory Fido. Lawrenceville, NJ: Africa World Press inc., 1990.

SHAKESPEARE, William. *The Riverside Shakespeare*. Boston: Houghton Mifflin Co., 1974.

SMITH, Huston. *Religions of Man*. New York: Harper and Row, 1964.

SOYINKA, Wole. *Myth, Literature and the African World*. Cambridge: Cambridge UP, 1976.

SPEIRS, Ronald. *Bertolt Brecht*. London: Macmillian Publishers Ltd., 1987.

ST OMER, Grath. *The Lights on the Hill*. London: Heinemann Educational Books Ltd., 1968.

TATE, Allen. *The Language of Poetry*. New York: Russell & Russell, 1960.

TAYLOR, Jeremy. *"The Joker of Seville – Actors Give Grand Performances."* Trinidad Express 4 December 1974: 9+

---. *"Walcott Mesmerizes and Dazzles Audience with his Language."* Trinidad Express 21 October 1974: 5.

THOMAS, J. J. *Froudacity West Indian Fables by James Anthony Froude Explained by J. J. Thomas*. London: New Beacon Books Ltd., 1889.

TILLYARD, E. M. W. *Some Mythical Elements in English Literature*. London: Chatto & Windus, 1961.

TYSON, George F. *Toussaint L'Ouverture*. Trenton, NJ: Prentice-Hall Inc., 1973.

VALDES, Mario J. *Phenomenological Hermeneutics and the Study of Literature*. Toronto: U of Toronto P, 1987.

VAN SERTIMA, Ivan. *They Came Before Columbus*. New York: Random House, 1976.

WALKER, Alice. *You Can't Keep a Good Woman Down*. London: The Women's Press, 1982.

---. *Possessing the Secret of Joy*. New York: Harcourt Brace Jovanovich, 1992.

WEINSTEIN, Brian and Aaron Segal. *Haiti: Political Failures, Cultural Successes.* New York: Praeger Publishers, 1984.

WHEELWRIGHT, PHILIP. *"Poetry, Myth, Reality."* The Language of Poetry. Ed. Allen Tate. New York: Russel & Russel, 1960. 3-36.

WILLIAMS, Eric. *History of the People of Trinidad and Tobago.* London: Andre Deutsch Ltd., 1964.

WILLIAMS Raymond. *Drama From Ibsen to Brecht.* London: Chatto & Windus Ltd., 1952.

---. *Marxism and Literature.* Oxford: Oxford UP, 1977.

WINTERS, Yvor. *The Function of Criticism.* London: Routledge Ltd., 1962.

WITVIET, Theo. *A Place in the Sun: An Introduction to Liberation Theology in the Third World.* London: SCM Press Ltd., 1985.

WOOD, Charles T. *Age of Chivalry: Manners and Morals 1000-1450.* London: Weidenfeld and Nicolson, 1970.

WYNTER, Syliva. Afterword. *"Beyond Miranda's Meaning: Un/Silencing the Demonic Ground of Caliban's Woman."* Out of the Kumbla. Caribbean Women Writers in Literature. Eds. Carol Boyce Davies and Elaine Savory Fido. Lawrenceville, NJ: Africa World Press Inc., 1990. 355-366.

YATES, Frances A. *Giordano Bruno and the Hermetic Tradition.* London Routledge, 1964.

www.ingramcontent.com/pod-product-compliance
Lightning Source LLC
Chambersburg PA
CBHW051826040426
42447CB00006B/382